The Blue Book of Grammar and Punctuation

Ninth Edition

THE BLUE BOOK
OF GRAMMAR AND PUNCTUATION

NINTH EDITION

THE MYSTERIES OF GRAMMAR AND PUNCTUATION REVEALED

AN EASY-TO-USE REFERENCE GUIDE AND WORKBOOK

JANE STRAUS

Straus, Jane

Library of Congress Control Number TX-4-702-146
The blue book of grammar and punctuation : an easy-to-use reference guide and workbook

ISBN 0-9667221-8-3

Book Design by Gary Klehr

Published by Jane Straus
P.O. Box 472
Mill Valley, California 94942
www.grammarbook.com
800-644-3222

Ordering information and quantity discounts

For easy ordering:
Call: 1 800 247 6553 / 419 281 1802
Fax: 419-281-6883
Email: order@bookmasters.com.
Online: www.grammarbook.com

Quantity discounts for classrooms, sales promotions,
corporate training, premiums, and fundraisers.

ABOUT THE BOOK

This entertaining and concise reference guide and workbook answers your most pressing questions about English usage. Jane has unraveled the mysteries of grammar, punctuation, and capitalization to help you feel competent in your writing and speaking skills. Tens of thousands of copies of this indispensable book are purchased worldwide every year by business professionals, government agencies, universities, high schools, middle schools, and homeschooling families.

You will discover why others can't wait to get their hands on the book when you look at the first page: easy-to-understand rules, abundant examples, and dozens of exercises with answers, offering you ample opportunity to practice your skills.

The first part of the book contains the most common rules of grammar and punctuation. The second part contains numerous practice exercises followed by answers to give you instant feedback on your comprehension and to help you build your confidence.

For each grammar topic and punctuation mark, you will find two sets of exercises. Additionally, you can get a valuable *before and after* picture by doing the comprehensive grammar and punctuation pretests and mastery tests.

For excerpts of the book, interactive quizzes, updated information, articles by the author, or to schedule a seminar, go to www.grammarbook.com

ABOUT THE AUTHOR

Author, seminar leader, personal coach, and talk show guest, Jane Straus has a gift for combining inspiration, entertainment, and education. She invites you to take a look at her self-help website, www.stopenduring.com, where you will find excerpts from her popular and powerful book, *Enough Is Enough! Stop Enduring and Start Living Your Extraordinary Life* (Jossey-Bass, 2005).

You will also find seminar and media video clips of Jane, testimonials about her work by famous writers as well as by seminar participants, and information about her coaching services.

GRAMMAR

PUNCTUATION

PUNCTUATION continued

TABLE OF CONTENTS: Exercises

FINDING SUBJECTS AND VERBS

Being able to find the right subject and verb will help you correct errors concerning agreement.

> *Example*   *The <u>list</u> of items <u>is</u>/are on the desk.*
> *If you know that* list *is the subject, then you will choose* is *for the verb.*

Being able to identify the subject and verb correctly will also help you with commas and semi-colons as you will see later.

<u>Definition</u>. A **Verb** is a word that shows action (runs, hits, slides) or state of being (is, are, was, were, am, etc.).

> *Examples*   *<u>He</u> <u>ran</u> around the block.*
> *<u>You</u> <u>are</u> my friend.*

<u>Rule 1</u>. If a verb follows *to*, it is called an infinitive phrase and is not the main verb. You will find the main verb either before or after the infinitive phrase.

> *Example*   *<u>I</u> <u>like</u> to walk.*
> *The <u>efforts</u> to get her elected <u>succeeded</u>.*

<u>Definition</u>. A **Subject** is the noun or pronoun that performs the verb.

> *Example*   *The <u>woman</u> <u>hurried</u>.* Woman *is the subject.*

<u>Rule 2</u>. A subject will come before a phrase beginning with *of*.

> *Example*   *A <u>bouquet</u> of yellow roses <u>will lend</u> color and fragrance to the room.*

FINDING SUBJECTS AND VERBS continued

<u>Rule 3</u>. To find the subject and verb, always find the verb first. Then ask who or what performed the verb.

    Examples   *The jet <u>engine</u> <u>passed</u> inspection.*
                          Passed is the verb. Who or what passed?
                          The *engine*, so *engine* is the subject.
                          If you included the word *jet* as the subject, lightning will not strike you.
                          Technically, jet is an adjective here and is part of what is known as the
                          complete subject.

                          *From the ceiling <u>**hung**</u> the <u>chandelier</u>.*
                          The verb is *hung*. Now, if you think *ceiling* is the subject, slow down.
                          Ask *who* or *what* hung. The answer is *chandelier*, not *ceiling*.
                          Therefore, *chandelier* is the subject.

<u>Rule 4</u>. Any request or command such as "Stop!" or "Walk quickly." has the understood subject *you* because if we ask who is to stop or walk quickly, the answer must be *you*.

    Example   *(<u>You</u>) Please <u>bring</u> me some coffee.*
                          Bring is the verb. Who is to do the bringing? *You* understood.

<u>Rule 5</u>. Sentences often have more than one subject, more than one verb, or pairs of subjects and verbs.

    Examples   *<u>I</u> <u>like</u> cake and <u>he</u> <u>likes</u> ice cream.*
                          Two pairs of subjects and verbs
                          <u>He</u> and <u>I</u> <u>like</u> cake.
                          Two subjects and one verb
                          <u>She</u> <u>lifts</u> weights and <u>jogs</u> daily.
                          One subject and two verbs

SUBJECT AND VERB AGREEMENT

Basic Rule. The basic rule states that a singular subject takes a singular verb while a plural subject takes a plural verb. The trick is in knowing whether the subject is singular or plural. The next trick is recognizing a singular or plural verb.

> **Hint:** Verbs do not form their plurals by adding an *s* as nouns do. In order to determine which verb is singular and which one is plural, think of which verb you would use with *he* or *she* and which verb you would use with *they*.

Example   *talks, talk*
Which one is the singular form? Which word would you use with *he*?
We say, "He talks." Therefore, *talks* is singular. We say, "They talk."
Therefore, *talk* is plural.

Rule 1. Two singular subjects connected by *or* or *nor* require a singular verb.

Example   *My <u>aunt</u> or my <u>uncle</u> <u>is arriving</u> by train today.*

Rule 2. Two singular subjects connected by either/or or neither/nor require a singular verb as in Rule 1.

Examples   *Neither <u>Juan</u> nor <u>Carmen</u> <u>is</u> available.*

                  Either <u>Kiana</u> or <u>Casey</u> <u>helps</u> today with stage decorations.

Rule 3. When one of your two subjects is *I*, put it second and follow it with the singular verb *am*.

Examples   *Neither <u>she</u> nor <u>I</u> <u>am going</u> to the festival.*

Rule 4. When a singular subject is connected by *or* or *nor* to a plural subject, put the plural subject last and use a plural verb.

Example   *The <u>book</u> or the <u>magazines</u> <u>are</u> on the shelf.*

Rule 5. When a singular and plural subject are connected by *either/or* or *neither/nor* put the plural subject last and use a plural verb.

Example   *Neither <u>Jenny</u> nor the <u>others</u> <u>are</u> available.*

Rule 6. As a general rule, use a plural verb with two or more subjects when they are connected by *and*.

Example   *A <u>car</u> and a <u>bike</u> <u>are</u> my means of transportation.*

SUBJECT AND VERB AGREEMENT continued

<u>Rule 7</u>. Sometimes the subject is separated from the verb by words such as *along with, as well as, besides,* or *not.* Ignore these expressions when determining whether to use a singular or plural verb.

Examples   *The <u>politician</u>, along with the newsmen, <u>is expected</u> shortly.*
              <u>Excitement</u>, as well as nervousness, <u>is</u> the cause of her shaking.

<u>Rule 8</u>. The pronouns *each, everyone, every one, everybody, anyone, anybody, someone,* and *somebody* are singular and require singular verbs. Do not be misled by what follows *of.*

Examples   *<u>Each</u> of the girls <u>sings</u> well.*
              Every <u>one</u> of the cakes <u>is</u> gone.

NOTE: *Everyone* is one word when it means *everybody. Every one* is two words when the meaning is *each one.*

<u>Rule 9</u>. With words that indicate portions—*percent, fraction, part, majority, some, all, none, remainder,* etc.—you must look at the noun in your *of phrase* (object of the preposition) to determine whether to use a singular or plural verb. If the object of the preposition is singular, use a singular verb. If the object of the preposition is plural, use a plural verb.

Examples   *<u>Fifty percent</u> of the pie <u>has</u> disappeared.*
              Pie is the object of the preposition of.

              <u>Fifty percent</u> of the pies <u>have</u> disappeared.
              Pies is the object of the preposition.

              <u>One third</u> of the city <u>is</u> unemployed.
              <u>One third</u> of the people <u>are</u> unemployed.

              <u>All</u> of the pie <u>is</u> gone.
              <u>All</u> of the pies <u>are</u> gone.

              <u>Some</u> of the pie <u>is missing.</u>
              <u>Some</u> of the pies <u>are missing.</u>

<u>Rule 10</u>. When *either* and *neither* are subjects, they always take singular verbs.

Example   *<u>Neither</u> of them <u>is</u> available to speak right now.*
             <u>Either</u> of us <u>is</u> capable of doing the job.

SUBJECT AND VERB AGREEMENT continued

<u>Rule 11</u>.   The words *here* and *there* are never subjects because they are not nouns. In sentences beginning with *here* or *there*, the true subject follows the verb.

  Examples   There <u>are</u> four <u>hurdles</u> to jump.
            There <u>is</u> a high <u>hurdle</u> to jump.

<u>Rule 12</u>.   Use a singular verb with sums of money or periods of time.

  Examples   Ten <u>dollars</u> <u>is</u> a high price to pay.
            Five <u>years</u> <u>is</u> the maximum sentence for that offense.

<u>Rule 13</u>.   Sometimes the pronoun *who, that,* or *which* is the subject of a verb in the middle of the sentence. The pronouns *who, that,* and *which* become singular or plural according to the noun directly in front of them. So, if that noun is singular, use a singular verb. If it is plural, use a plural verb.

  Examples   *Salma is the scientist <u>who</u> <u>writes</u>/write the reports.*
            The word in front of who is *scientist*, which is singular. Therefore, use the singular verb *writes*.

            He is one of the men <u>who</u> does/<u>do</u> the work.
            The word in front of *who* is *men*, which is plural. Therefore, use the plural verb *do*.

<u>Rule 14</u>.   Collective nouns such as *team* and *staff* may be either singular or plural depending on their use in the sentence.

  Examples   *The <u>staff</u> <u>is</u> in a meeting.*
            Staff is acting as a unit here.

            The <u>staff</u> <u>are</u> in disagreement about the findings.
            The staff are acting as separate individuals in this example. The sentence would read even better as:
            The staff <u>members</u> <u>are</u> in disagreement about the findings.

PRONOUNS

<u>Definition</u>. A **pronoun** is a word that takes the place of a noun. Pronouns can be in one of three cases: Subject, Object, or Possessive.

<u>Rule 1</u>. Subject pronouns are used when the pronoun is the subject of the sentence. You can remember subject pronouns easily by filling in the blank subject space for a simple sentence.

Example _____ *did the job.*
I, you, he, she, it, we, and *they* all fit into the blank and are, therefore, subject pronouns.

<u>Rule 2</u>. Subject pronouns are also used if they rename the subject. They will follow to be verbs such as is, are, was, were, am, and will be.

Examples *It is he.*
This is she speaking.
It is we who are responsible for the decision to downsize.

NOTE: In spoken English, most people tend to follow *to be* verbs with object pronouns. Many English teachers support (or at least have given in to) this distinction between written and spoken English.

Example *It could have been them.*
Better *It could have been they.*

Example *It is just me at the door.*
Better *It is just I at the door.*

<u>Rule 3</u>. Object pronouns are used everywhere else (direct object, indirect object, object of the preposition). Object pronouns are me, you, him, her, it, us, and them.

Examples *Jean talked to him.*
Are you talking to me?

<u>Rule 4</u>. To be able to choose pronouns correctly, you must learn to identify clauses. A clause is a group of words containing a verb and subject. A **strong clause** can stand on its own.

Examples <u>She</u> <u>is</u> *hungry.*
<u>I</u> <u>am feeling</u> *well today.*

PRONOUNS continued

Rule 4a. A **weak clause** begins with words such as *although, since, if, when,* and *because.* Weak clauses cannot stand on their own.

Examples *Although she is hungry . . .*
If she is hungry . . .
Since I am feeling well...

Rule 4b. If a sentence contains more than one clause, isolate the clauses so that you can decide which pronoun is correct.

	WEAK	STRONG
Examples	*[Although she is hungry,]*	*[she will give him some of her food.]*
	[Although this gift is for him,]	*[I would like you to have it too.]*

Rule 5. To decide whether to use the Subject or Object pronoun after the words than or as, mentally complete the sentence.

Examples *Thinh is as smart as she/her.*
If we mentally complete the sentence, we would say, "Thinh is as smart as she is." Therefore, *she* is the correct answer.

Zoe is taller than I/me.
Mentally completing the sentence, we have, "Zoe is taller than I am."

Daniel would rather talk to her than I/me.
We can mentally complete this sentence in two ways: *Daniel would rather talk to her than to me.* **OR** *Daniel would rather talk to her than I would.* As you can see, the meaning will change depending on the pronoun you choose.

Rule 6. Possessive Pronouns show ownership and never need apostrophes.
Possessive Pronouns: mine, yours, his, hers, its, ours, theirs

NOTE: The only time *it's* has an apostrophe is when it is a contraction for *it is.*

Examples *It's a cold morning.*
The thermometer reached its highest reading.

PRONOUNS continued

<u>Rule 7</u>. The following examples demonstrate pitfalls to avoid when using possessive pronouns.

Correct	*Not <u>one</u> of the neighbors <u>offered</u> his/her support.*
	<u>None</u> of the neighbors <u>offered</u> their support.
	Remember that *none* is a portion word and becomes singular or plural depending on the noun after *of* (the object of the preposition). *None* is plural here because of the plural *neighbors*.
Incorrect	*Not <u>one</u> of the neighbors <u>offered</u> their support.*

<u>Rule 8</u>. Reflexive pronouns—*myself, himself, herself, itself, themselves, ourselves, yourself, yourselves*—should be used only when they refer back to another word in the sentence.

Correct	*I did it myself.*
Incorrect	*My brother and myself did it.*
	The word *myself* does not refer back to another word.
Correct	*My brother and I did it.*
Incorrect	*Please give it to John or myself.*
Correct	*Please give it to John or me.*

WHO vs. WHOM

<u>Rule.</u> Use the he/him method to decide which word is correct.

he = who
him = whom

Examples   ***Who****/Whom wrote the letter?*
He wrote the letter. Therefore, *who* is correct.

*For who/****whom*** *should I vote?*
Should I vote for him? Therefore, *whom* is correct.

We all know ***who****/whom pulled that prank.*
This sentence contains two clauses: *We all know* and *who/whom pulled that prank.* We are interested in the second clause because it contains the *who/whom. He* pulled that prank. Therefore, *who* is correct.
(Are you starting to sound like a hooting owl yet?)

*We want to know on who/****whom*** *the prank was pulled.*
This sentence contains two clauses: *We want to know* and *the prank was pulled on who/whom.* Again, we are interested in the second clause because it contains the who/whom. The prank was pulled on him. Therefore, *whom* is correct.

WHOEVER vs. WHOMEVER

<u>Rule 1</u>. First of all, use the *ever* suffix when *who* or *whom* can fit into two clauses in the sentence.

Example   *Give it to* ***whoever****/whomever asks for it first.*
Give it to *him. He* asks for it first.

<u>Rule 2</u>. Because we can substitute him and he into both clauses, we must use the ever suffix. Now, to determine whether to use whoever or whomever, here is the rule:

him + he = whoever
him + him = whomever
Therefore, *Give it to whoever asks for it first.*

Example   *We will hire whoever/****whomever*** *you recommend.*
We will hire *him.* You recommend *him.*
him + him = whomever

Example   *We will hire* ***whoever****/whomever is most qualified.*
We will hire *him. He* is most qualified.
him + he = whoever

THAT vs. WHICH

Rule 1. *Who* refers to people. *That* and *which* refer to groups or things.

Examples   Anya is the one **who** rescued the bird.
Lokua is on the team **that** won first place.
She belongs to an organization **that** specializes in saving endangered species.

Rule 2. *That* introduces essential clauses while *which* introduces nonessential clauses.

Examples   I do not trust editorials **that** claim racial differences in intelligence.
We would not know which editorials were being discussed without the *that* clause.

The editorial claiming racial differences in intelligence, **which** appeared in the Sunday newspaper, upset me.
The editorial is already identified. Therefore, *which* begins a nonessential clause.

NOTE: Essential clauses do not have commas surrounding them while nonessential clauses do contain commas.

Rule 3. If *this*, *that*, *these*, or *those* has already introduced an essential clause, use *which* to introduce the next clause, whether it is essential or nonessential.

Examples   **That** is a decision **which** you must live with for the rest of your life.
Those ideas, **which** we've discussed thoroughly enough, do not need to be addressed again.

NOTE: Often, you can streamline your sentence by leaving out *which*.

Example   **Those** ideas, **which** we have discussed thoroughly, do not need to be addressed again.

Better   The ideas we have discussed thoroughly do not need to be addressed again.

Example   **That** is a decision **which** you must live with for the rest of your life.

Better   **That** is a decision you must live with for the rest of your life.

ADJECTIVES AND ADVERBS

Definitions   Adjectives are words that describe nouns or pronouns. They may come before the word they describe (That is a cute puppy.) or they may follow the word they describe (That puppy is cute.).

Adverbs are words that modify everything but nouns and pronouns. They modify adjectives, verbs, and other adverbs. A word is an adverb if it answers how, when, or where.

The only adverbs that cause grammatical problems are those that answer the question how, so we will focus on these.

Example   *He speaks **slowly**.*
Answers the question how.

Example   *He speaks **very slowly**.*
Answers the question how slowly.

Rule 1. Generally, if a word answers the question *how*, it is an adverb. If it can have an *ly* added to it, place it there.

Examples   *She thinks slow/**slowly**.*
She thinks how? slowly.

*She is a **slow**/slowly thinker.*
Slow does not answer *how* so no *ly* is attached. *Slow* is an adjective here.

*She thinks **fast**/fastly.*
Fast answers the question *how*, so it is an adverb. But *fast* never has an *ly* attached to it.

*We performed bad/**badly**.*
Badly describes how we performed.

ADJECTIVES AND ADVERBS continued

<u>Rule 2</u>. A special *ly* rule applies when four of the senses—*taste, smell, look, feel*—are the verbs. Do not ask if these senses answer the question *how* to determine if *ly* should be attached. Instead, ask if the sense verb is being used actively. If so, use the *ly*.

> *Examples*   *Roses smell **sweet**/sweetly.*
> Do the roses actively smell with noses? No, so no *ly*.
>
> *The woman looked **angry**/angrily.*
> Did the woman actively look with eyes or are we describing her appearance? We are only describing appearance, so no *ly*.
>
> *The woman looked angry/**angrily** at the paint splotches.*
> Here the woman did actively look with eyes so the *ly* was added.
>
> *She feels **bad**/badly about the news.*
> She is not feeling with fingers, so no *ly*.

<u>Rule 3</u>. The word *good* is an adjective while *well* is an adverb.

> *Examples*   *You did a good job.*
> *Good* describes the job.
>
> *You did the job well.*
> *Well* answers how.
>
> *You smell good today.*
> Describes your odor, not how you smell with your nose, so follow with the adjective.
>
> *You smell well for someone with a cold.*
> You are actively smelling with a nose here so follow with the adverb.

<u>Rule 4.</u> When referring to health, always use *well*.

> *Examples*   *I do not feel well.*
>
> *You do not look well today.*

ADJECTIVES AND ADVERBS continued

<u>Rule 5</u>. A common error in using adjectives and adverbs arises from using the wrong form for comparison. For instance, to describe one thing we would say *poor*, as in, "She is *poor*." To compare two things, we should say *poorer*, as in, "She is the *poorer* of the two women." To compare more than two things, we should say *poorest*, as in, "She is the *poorest* of them all."

Examples	**One**	**Two**	**Three or More**
	sweet	*sweeter*	*sweetest*
	bad	*worse*	*worst*
	efficient*	*more efficient**	*most efficient**

*Usually with words of three or more syllables, don't add -er or -est. Use more or most in front of the words.

<u>Rule 6</u>. Never drop the *ly* from an adverb when using the comparison form.

Correct	*She spoke quickly.*
	She spoke more quickly than he did.
Incorrect	*She spoke quicker than he did.*
Correct	*Talk quietly.*
	Talk more quietly.
Incorrect	*Talk quieter.*

<u>Rule 7</u>. When *this, that, these,* and *those* are followed by nouns, they are adjectives. When they appear without a noun following them, they are pronouns.

Examples	*This house is for sale.*
	This is an adjective here.
	This is for sale.
	This is a pronoun here.

<u>Rule 8</u>. *This* and *that* are singular, whether they are being used as adjectives or as pronouns. *This* points to something nearby while *that* points to something "over there."

Examples	*This dog is mine.*
	That dog is hers.
	This is mine.
	That is hers.

ADJECTIVES AND ADVERBS continued

<u>Rule 9</u>. *These* and *those* are plural, whether they are being used as adjectives or as pronouns. *These* points to something nearby while *those* points to something "over there."

  Examples   *These babies have been smiling for a long time.*
         These are mine.
         Those babies have been crying for hours.
         Those are yours.

<u>Rule 10</u>. Use *than* to show comparison. Use *then* to answer the question *when*.

  Examples   *I would rather go skiing than rock climbing.*
         First we went skiing; then we went rock climbing.

PROBLEMS WITH PREPOSITIONS

<u>Rule 1</u>. You may end a sentence with a preposition. Just <u>do not use extra</u> prepositions when the meaning is clear without them.

  Examples
  Correct   *That is something I cannot agree with.*
       OR
       That is something with <u>which</u> I cannot agree.

  Correct   *How many of you can I count on?*

  Correct   *Where did he go?*
  Incorrect *Where did he go to?*

  Correct   *Where did you get this?*
  Incorrect *Where did you get this at?*

  Correct   *I will go later.*
  Incorrect *I will go later on.*

  Correct   *Take your shoes off the bed.*
  Incorrect *Take your shoes off of the bed.*

  Correct   *You may look out the window.*
  Incorrect *You may look out of the window.*

  Correct   *Cut it into small pieces.*
  Incorrect *Cut it up into small pieces.*

PROBLEMS WITH PREPOSITIONS continued

Rule 2. Use *on* with expressions that indicate the time of an occurrence.

> *Examples*   *He was born on December 23.*
> *We will arrive on the fourth.*

Rule 3. *Of* should never be used in place of *have.*

> *Correct*   *I should have done it.*
> *Incorrect*   *I should of done it.*

Rule 4. *Between* refers to two. *Among* is used for three or more.

> *Examples*   *Divide the candy between the two of you.*
> *Divide the candy among the three of you.*

Rule 5. *Into* implies entrance; *in* does not.

> *Examples*   *Sofia walked into the house.*
> *Sofia was waiting in the house.*
> *Miriam came in to see me today.*
>
> *In* is part of the verb phrase *came in* while *to* is part of *to see.*

Rule 6. The word *like*, when used to show comparison, is a preposition, meaning that it should be followed by an object of the preposition but not by a subject and verb. Use the connectors (also called conjunctions) *as* or *as if* when following a comparison with a subject and verb.

> *Examples*   *You look so much like your mother.*
> Mother is the object of the preposition *like.*
>
> *You look as if you are angry.*
> *As if* is connecting two pairs of subjects and verbs.

EFFECT vs. AFFECT

<u>Rule 1</u>. Use *effect* when you mean *bring about* or *brought about, cause* or *caused.*

> *Example*   *He effected a commotion in the crowd.*
> *Meaning:*   *He caused a commotion in the crowd.*

<u>Rule 2</u>. Use *effect* when you mean *result.*

> *Example*   *What effect did that speech have?*

<u>Rule 3</u>. Also use *effect* whenever any of these words precede it:
>   a   an   any   the   take   into   no
>   NOTE: These words may be separated from *effect* by an adjective.

> *Examples*   *That book had a long-lasting effect on my thinking.*
> *Has the medicine produced any noticeable effects?*

<u>Rule 4</u>. Use the verb *affect* when you mean *to influence* rather than *to cause.*

> *Example*   *How do the budget cuts affect your staffing?*

<u>Rule 5</u>. *Affect* is used as a noun to mean emotional expression.

> *Example*   *She showed little affect when told she had won the lottery.*

LIE vs. LAY

You will impress your friends with your grammar skills if you can distinguish between *lie* and *lay*. Use this chart as a handy reference.

Lie vs. Lay Chart

	Present	Past	Participle (a form of have)
To recline	lie, lying	lay	has/have/had lain
To put or place (verb followed by an object)	lay, laying	laid	has/have/had laid
To tell a falsehood	lie, lying	lied	has/have/had lied

Examples in Present Tense	*I like to lie down for a nap at 2:00 p.m.*
	I am lying down for a nap today.
	The hens lay eggs.
	The hen is laying eggs.
	I am tempted to lie about my age.
	I am not lying about my age.
Examples in Past Tense	*I lay down for a nap yesterday at 2:00 p.m.*
	The hen laid two eggs yesterday.
	He lied on the witness stand.
Examples with a Participle	*I have lain down for a nap every day this week.*
	The hen has laid two eggs every day this week.
	He has lied each day on the witness stand.

EFFECTIVE WRITING

<u>Rule 1</u>. Use concrete rather than vague language.

Examples   *Vague:*   *The weather was of an extreme nature on the west coast.*
           Concrete: *California had very cold weather last week.*

<u>Rule 2</u>. Use active voice whenever possible. Active voice means the subject is performing the verb.

Examples   *Active:*   *Barry hit the ball.*
           Passive: *The ball was hit.*

           Notice that the responsible party may not even appear when using passive voice.

<u>Rule 3</u>. Avoid overusing *there is, there are, it is, it was,* etc.

Example   *There is a case of meningitis that was reported in the newspaper.*
Correction   *A case of meningitis was reported in the newspaper.*
Even Better   *The newspaper reported a case of meningitis.* (Active voice)

Example   *It is important to signal before making a left turn.*
Correction   *Signaling before making a left turn is important.* **OR**
           Signaling before a left turn is important. **OR**
           You should signal before making a left turn. (Active voice)

Example   *There are some revisions which must be made.*
Correction   *Some revisions must be made.*
Even Better   *Please make some revisions.* (Active voice)

<u>Rule 4</u>. To avoid confusion, don't use two negatives to make a positive.

Incorrect   *He is not unwilling to help.*
Correct   *He is willing to help.*

<u>Rule 5</u>. Use similar grammatical form when offering several ideas. This is called parallel construction.

Correct   *You should check your spelling, grammar, and punctuation.*
Incorrect   *You should check your spelling, grammar, and punctuating.*

EFFECTIVE WRITING continued

<u>Rule 6</u>. If you start a sentence with an action, place the actor immediately after or you will have created the infamous dangling modifier.

> *Incorrect*   *While walking across the street, the bus hit her.*
>
> *Correct*   *While walking across the street, she was hit by a bus.*
>
> **OR**
>
> *She was hit by a bus while walking across the street.*

<u>Rule 7</u>. Place modifiers near the words they modify.

> *Incorrect*   *I have some pound cake Mollie baked in my lunch bag.*
>
> *Correct*   *In my lunch bag, I have some pound cake that Mollie baked.*

<u>Rule 8</u>. A sentence fragment occurs when you have only a phrase or weak clause but are missing a strong clause.

> *Example of Sentence Fragment*   *After the show ended.*
>
> *Example of Sentence*   *After the show ended, we got a cup of coffee.*

SPACING WITH PUNCTUATION

<u>Rule 1</u>. With a typewriter, you sometimes use one space or two spaces following punctuation. With a computer, use only one space following periods, commas, semicolons, colons, exclamation points, question marks, and quotation marks. With a computer, the space needed after these punctuation marks is proportioned automatically.

<u>Rule 2</u>. Use no spaces on either side of a hyphen. [For more rules about hyphens, see page 38.]

    Example   *We borrowed twenty-three sheets of paper.*

NOTE: For spacing with ellipsis marks, see below. For spacing with en and em dashes, see page 43.

PERIODS

<u>Rule 1</u>. Use a period at the end of a complete sentence that is a statement.

    Example   *I know that you would never break my trust intentionally.*

<u>Rule 2</u>. If the last word in the sentence ends in a period, do not follow it with another period.

    Examples   *I know that M.D. She is my sister-in-law.*
                    Please shop, cook, etc. I will do the laundry.

<u>Rule 3</u>. Use the period after an indirect question.

    Example   *He asked where his suitcase was.*

ELLIPSIS MARKS

NOTE: To create ellipsis marks with a PC, hit space, period, space, period, space, period, space. On a Mac, hit Option Semicolon.

<u>Rule 1</u>. If words are omitted at the end of a quoted sentence, use ellipsis marks followed by the necessary ending punctuation mark.

    Examples   *The regulation states, "All agencies must document overtime . . . ."*
                 The original sentence read, *The regulation states, "All agencies must document overtime or risk losing federal funds."*

                 She said, "Can you tell me what happened to . . . ?"

ELLIPSIS MARKS continued

<u>Rule 2</u>. Sometimes sentences are meant to trail off. Use ellipsis marks without any ending punctuation in this situation.

       Example   *"I thought that you might . . ."*

<u>Rule 3</u>. If words are omitted within a quoted sentence, use ellipsis marks where you have left out the word(s).

       Example   *"According to our records, Callan received . . . awards for best actress."*

       Original   *"According to our records, Callan received two Emmys and two Oscar awards for best actress."*

<u>Rule 4</u>. If sentences are omitted between other sentences within a quotation, use ellipsis marks after the ending punctuation mark of the preceding sentence.

       Example   *The regulation states, "Agencies may risk losing federal funds. . . . All agencies will be audited annually."*

    NOTE: The first period has no space before it because it is the ending punctuation mark for the first sentence. After the ellipsis marks, one space follows before the next sentence.

<u>Rule 5</u>. If your quoted material begins with the middle of a sentence, use the ellipsis marks at the beginning of the quotation.

       Example   *Abraham Lincoln, in his Gettysburg address, said, ". . . our fathers brought forth . . . a new nation, conceived in liberty, and dedicated to the proposition that 'all men are created equal.'"*

    NOTE: The second set of ellipsis marks in the above example is used where words within the quoted sentence have been omitted.

    The original reads, *"Four score and seven years ago our fathers brought forth, upon this continent, a new nation, conceived in liberty, and dedicated to the proposition that 'all men are created equal.'"*

<u>Rule 6</u>. When you omit one or more paragraphs within a long quotation, use ellipsis marks after the last punctuation mark that ends the preceding paragraph.

COMMAS

Rule 1. To avoid confusion, use commas to separate words and word groups with a series of three or more.

> *Example* *My $10,000,000 estate is to be split among my husband, daughter, son, and nephew.*

> **NOTE:** Omitting the comma after son would indicate that the son and nephew would have to split one-third of the estate.

Rule 2. Use a comma to separate two adjectives when the word *and* can be inserted between them.

> *Examples* *He is a strong, healthy man.*
> *We stayed at an expensive summer resort.*
> You would not say *expensive and summer resort,* so no comma.

Rule 3. Use a comma when an *ly* adjective is used with other adjectives.

> **NOTE:** To test if an *ly* word is an adjective, see if it can be used alone with the noun. If it can, use the comma.

> *Examples* *Felix was a lonely, young boy.*
>
> *I get headaches in brightly lit rooms.*
>
> *Brightly* is not an adjective because it cannot be used alone with *rooms*; therefore, no comma is used between *brightly* and *lit.*

Rule 4. Use commas before or surrounding the name or title of a person directly addressed.

> *Examples* *Will you, Aisha, do that assignment for me?*
> *Yes, Doctor, I will.*

> **NOTE:** Capitalize a title when directly addressing someone.

COMMAS continued

Rule 5a. Use a comma to separate the day of the month from the year and after the year.

> *Example*   *Kathleen met her husband on December 5, 2003, in Mill Valley, California.*

Rule 5b. If any part of the date is omitted, leave out the comma.

> *Example*   *They met in December 2003 in Mill Valley.*

Rule 6. Use a comma to separate the city from the state and after the state. Some businesses no longer use the comma after the state.

> *Example*   *I lived in San Francisco, California, for 20 years.*
> **OR**
> *I lived in San Francisco, California for 20 years.*

Rule 7. Use commas to surround degrees or titles used with names.

> *Example*   *Al Mooney, M.D., knew Sam Sunny, Jr.*

> **NOTE:** Sometimes people having names with *Jr.* attached do not use a comma before the *Jr.* If they do not use the comma, then you should not.

Rule 8. Use commas to set off expressions that interrupt the flow of the sentence.

> *Example*   *I am, as you have probably noticed, very nervous about this.*

Rule 9. When starting a sentence with a weak clause, use a comma after it. Conversely, do not use a comma when the sentence starts with a strong clause followed by a weak clause.

> *Examples*   *If you are not sure about this, let me know now.*
> *Let me know now if you are not sure about this.*

Rule 10. Use a comma after phrases of more than three words that begin a sentence.

> *Examples*   *To apply for this job, you must have previous experience.*
> *On February 14 many couples give each other candy or flowers.*

COMMAS continued

<u>Rule 11</u>. If something or someone is sufficiently identified, the description following it is considered nonessential and should be surrounded by commas.

    Examples   *Freddy, who has a limp, was in an auto accident.*
                          Freddy is named so the description is not essential.

                          The boy who has a limp was in an auto accident.
                          We do not know which boy is being referred to without further description; therefore, no commas are used.

<u>Rule 12</u>. Use a comma to separate two strong clauses joined by a coordinating conjunction—*and, or, but, for, nor.* You can omit the comma if the clauses are both short.

    Examples   *I have painted the entire house, but he is still working on sanding the doors.*
                          I paint and he writes.

<u>Rule 13</u>. Use the comma to separate two sentences if it will help avoid confusion.

    Example   *I chose the colors red and green, and blue was his first choice.*

<u>Rule 14</u>. A comma splice is an error caused by joining two strong clauses with only a comma instead of separating the clauses with a conjunction, a semicolon, or a period. A comma splice creates what is known as a run-on sentence.

    Incorrect   *Time flies when we are having fun, we are always having fun.*
                         (Comma splice)

    Correct   *Time flies when we are having fun and we are always having fun.*
                         Time flies when we are having fun; we are always having fun.
                         Time flies when we are having fun. We are always having fun.

<u>Rule 15</u>. If the subject does not appear in front of the second verb, do not use a comma.

    Example   <u>He</u> <u>thought</u> *quickly when asked that difficult question but still* <u>did</u> *not* <u>answer</u> *correctly.*

COMMAS continued

<u>Rule 16</u>. Use commas to introduce or interrupt direct quotations shorter than three lines.

    Examples   *He actually said, "I do not care."*

                             "Why," I asked, "do you always forget to do it?"

<u>Rule 17</u>. Use a comma to separate a statement from a question.

    Example   *I can go, can't I?*

<u>Rule 18</u>. Use a comma to separate contrasting parts of a sentence.

    Example   *That is my money, not yours.*

<u>Rule 19</u>. Use a comma when beginning sentences with introductory words such as *well, now,* or *yes.*

    Examples   *Yes, I do need that report.*

                             Well, I never thought I'd live to see the day . . .

<u>Rule 20</u>. Use commas surrounding words such as *therefore* and *however* when they are used as interruptors.

    Examples   *I would, therefore, like a response.*

                             I would be happy, however, to volunteer for the Red Cross.

<u>Rule 21</u>. It is preferable to use a comma, not a semicolon, before introductory words such as *namely, that is, i.e., for example, e.g.,* or *for instance* when they are followed by a series of items. The comma after the introductory word is optional.

    Examples   *You may be required to bring many items, e.g., sleeping bags, pans, and warm clothing.*

                             As we discussed, you will bring two items, i.e. a sleeping bag and a tent.

SEMICOLONS

<u>Rule 1</u>. You may use a semicolon in place of a period to separate two sentences where the conjunction has been left out.

    Examples   *Call me tomorrow; I will give you my answer then.*

                        I have paid my dues; therefore, I expect all the privileges listed in the contract.

<u>Rule 2</u>. It is preferable to use a semicolon before introductory words such as *namely, that is, i.e., for example, e.g.,* or *for instance* when they introduce a complete sentence. It is also preferable to use the comma after the introductory word.

    Examples   *You may be required to bring many items; e.g., sleeping bags, pans, and warm clothing will make the trip better.*

                        As we discussed, you will bring two items; i.e., a sleeping bag and a tent are not optional.

    NOTE: *i.e.* means *that is*
              e.g. means *for example*

<u>Rule 3</u>. Use the semicolon to separate units of a series when one or more of the units contain commas.

    Example   *This conference has people that have come from Boise, Idaho; Los Angeles, California; and Nashville, Tennessee.*

<u>Rule 4</u>. Use the semicolon between two sentences that are joined by a conjunction but already have one or more commas within the first sentence.

    Examples   *When I finish here, I will be glad to help you; and that is a promise I will keep.*

                        If she can, she will attempt that feat; and if her husband is able, he will be there to see her.

COLONS

<u>Rule 1</u>. Use the colon after a complete sentence to introduce a list of items when introductory words such as *namely, for example,* or *that is* do not appear.

> *Examples*   *You may be required to bring many items: sleeping bags, pans, and warm clothing.*
>
> *I want the following items: butter, sugar, and flour.*
>
> *I want an assistant who can do the following: 1) input data, 2) write reports, and 3) complete tax forms.*

<u>Rule 2</u>. A colon should not precede a list unless it follows a complete sentence; however, the colon is a style choice that some publications allow.

> *Examples*   *If a waitress wants to make a good impression on her customers and boss, she should
> a) dress appropriately,
> b) calculate the bill carefully, and
> c) be courteous to customers.*
>
> *There are three ways a waitress can make a good impression on her boss and her customers:
> a) Dress appropriately.
> b) Calculate the bill carefully.
> c) Be courteous to customers.*
>
> *I want an assistant who can 1) input data, 2) write reports, and 3) complete tax forms.*

<u>Rule 3</u>. Capitalization and punctuation are optional when using single words or phrases in bulleted form. If each bullet or numbered point is a complete sentence, capitalize the first word and end each sentence with proper ending punctuation. The rule of thumb is to be consistent.

> *Examples*   *I want an assistant who can do the following:
> a) input data,
> b) write reports, and
> c) complete tax forms.*
>
> *The following are requested:
> a) Wool sweaters for possible cold weather.
> b) Wet suits for snorkeling.
> c) Introductions to the local dignitaries.*

COLONS continued

> *These are some of the pool rules:*
> *1. You must not run.*
> *2. If you see unsafe behavior, report it to the lifeguard.*
> *3. Have fun!*

<u>Rule 4</u>. Use a colon instead of a semicolon between two strong clauses (sentences) when the second clause explains or illustrates the first clause and no coordinating conjunction is being used to connect the clauses. Capitalization of the sentence following the colon is optional.

    Examples   *I enjoy reading: novels by Kurt Vonnegut are among my favorites.*
                                Garlic is used in Italian cooking: it greatly enhances the flavor of pasta dishes.

<u>Rule 5</u>. Use the colon to introduce a direct quotation that is more than three typewritten lines in length. In this situation, leave a blank line above and below the quoted material. Single space the long quotation. Some style manuals say to indent one-half inch on both the left and right margins; others say to indent only on the left margin. Quotation marks are not used.

<u>Rule 6</u>. Use the colon to follow the salutation of a business letter even when addressing someone by his/her first name. Never use a semicolon after a salutation. A comma is used after the salutation for personal correspondence.

QUESTION MARKS

<u>Rule 1</u>. Use a question mark only after a direct question.

    Examples   *Will you go with me?*
                                  I asked if he would go with me.

<u>Rule 2</u>. Use a question mark when a sentence is half statement and half question.

    Example   *You do care, don't you?*

EXCLAMATION POINTS

<u>Rule</u>. Use exclamation points to show emphasis or surprise. Do not use the exclamation point in formal business letters.

    Example   *I'm truly shocked by your behavior!*

QUOTATION MARKS

<u>Rule 1</u>. Periods and commas always go inside quotation marks, even inside single quotes.

Examples　　　*The sign changed from "Walk," to "Don't Walk," to "Walk" again within 30 seconds.*

She said, "Hurry up."

She said, "He said, 'Hurry up.'"

<u>Rule 2</u>. The placement of question marks with quotes follows logic. If a question is in quotation marks, the question mark should be placed inside the quotation marks.

Examples　　　*She asked, "Will you still be my friend?"*

Do you agree with the saying, "All's fair in love and war"?
Here the question is outside the quote.

NOTE: Only one ending punctuation mark is used with quotation marks. Also, the stronger punctuation mark wins. Therefore, no period after *war* is used.

<u>Rule 3</u>. When you have a question outside quoted material AND inside quoted material, use only one question mark and place it inside the quotation mark.

Example　　　*Did she say, "May I go?"*

<u>Rule 4</u>. Use single quotation marks for quotes within quotes. Note that the period goes inside all quote marks.

Example　　　*He said, "Danea said, 'Do not treat me that way.'"*

<u>Rule 5</u>. Use quotation marks to set off a direct quotation only.

Examples　　　*"When will you be here?" he asked.*

He asked when you will be there.

<u>Rule 6</u>. Do not use quotation marks with quoted material that is more than three lines in length. See Colons, Rule 5, p.39 for style guidance with longer quotes.

QUOTATION MARKS continued

<u>Rule 7</u>. When you are quoting something that has a spelling or grammar mistake or presents material in a confusing way, insert the term *sic* in italics and enclose it in brackets. *Sic* means, "This is the way the original material was."

    Example   *She wrote, "I would rather die then [sic] be seen wearing the same outfit as my sister."*

                        Should be *than*, not *then*.

PARENTHESES

<u>Rule 1</u>. Use parentheses to enclose words or figures that clarify or are used as an aside.

    Examples   *I expect five hundred dollars ($500).*

                        He finally answered (after taking five minutes to think) that he did not understand the question.
Commas could have been used in the above example. Parentheses show less emphasis or importance. Em dashes (see page 43), which could also have been used instead of parentheses, show emphasis.

<u>Rule 2</u>. You may use half parentheses to enclose numbers of listed items in a sentence.

    Example   *We need an emergency room physician who can 1) think quickly, 2) treat patients respectfully, and 3) handle complaints from the public.*

<u>Rule 3</u>. Periods go inside parentheses only if an entire sentence is inside the parentheses.

    Examples   *Please read the analysis (I enclosed it as Attachment A.).*
                        OR
                        Please read the analysis. (I enclosed it as Attachment A.)
                        OR
                        Please read the analysis (Attachment A).

APOSTROPHES

<u>Rule 1</u>. Use the apostrophe with contractions. The apostrophe is always placed at the spot where the letter(s) has been removed.

> *Examples*   *don't, isn't*
> *You're right.*
> *She's a great teacher.*

<u>Rule 2</u>. Use the apostrophe to show possession. Place the apostrophe before the *s* to show singular possession.

> *Examples*   *one boy's hat*
> *one woman's hat*
> *one actress's hat*
> *one child's hat*
> *Ms. Chang's house*
> *Mr. Jones's golf clubs*
> *Texas's weather*
> *Ms. Straus's daughter*
> *Jose Sanchez's artwork*
> *Dr. Hastings's appointment* (name is Hastings)
> *Mrs. Lees's books* (name is Lees)

<u>Rule 3</u>. To show plural possession, make the noun plural first. Then immediately use the apostrophe.

> *Examples*
> *two boys' hats*
> *two women's hats*
> *two actresses' hats*
> *two children's hats*
> *the Changs' house*
> *the Joneses' golf clubs*
> *the Strauses' daughter*
> *the Sanchezes' artwork*
> *the Hastingses' appointment*
> *the Leeses' books*

APOSTROPHES continued

<u>Rule 4</u>. With a singular compound noun, show possession with 's at the end of the word.

> *Example*   *my mother-in-law's hat.*

<u>Rule 5</u>. If the compound noun is plural, form the plural first and then use the apostrophe.

> *Example*   *my two brothers-in-law's hats*

<u>Rule 6</u>. Use the apostrophe and *s* after the second name only if two people possess the same item.

> *Examples*   *Cesar and Maribel's home is constructed of redwood.*
>
> *Cesar's and Maribel's job contracts will be renewed next year.*
> There is separate ownership.
>
> *Cesar and Maribel's job contracts will be renewed next year.*
> There is joint ownership of more than one contract.

<u>Rule 7</u>. Never use an apostrophe with possessive pronouns: *his, hers, its, theirs, ours, yours, whose.* They already show possession so they do not require an apostrophe. The only time an apostrophe is used for *it's* is when it is a contraction for *it is.*

> *Examples*   *This book is hers, not yours.*
> *It hurt its paw.*
> *It's a nice day.*
> *It's your right to refuse the invitation.*

<u>Rule 8</u>. The plurals for capital letters and numbers used as nouns are not formed with apostrophes.

> *Examples*   *She consulted with three M.D.s.*
> **BUT**
> *She went to three M.D.s' offices.*
> The apostrophe is needed here to show plural possessive.
> *She learned her ABCs.*
> *the 1990s* **not** *the 1990's*
> *the '90s or the mid-'70s* **not** *the '90's or the mid-'70's*
> *She learned her times tables for 6s and 7s.*

APOSTROPHES continued

Rule 9. Use possessive case in front of a gerund (*ing* word).

   Examples   *Alex's skating was a joy to behold.*
                     This does not stop Joan's inspecting of our facilities next Thursday.

Rule 10. If the gerund has a pronoun in front of it, use the possessive form of that pronoun.

   Examples   *I appreciate your inviting me to dinner.*
                     I appreciated his working with me to resolve the conflict.

HYPHENS

Authorities disagree on hyphenation more than on any other punctuation mark. Also, there are just too many rules for one human being to learn. Therefore, the following rules should be considered as guidelines only.

Hyphens Between Words

<u>Rule 1</u>. To check if a compound noun is two words, one word, or hyphenated, you may need to look it up in the dictionary. If you can't find the word in the dictionary, treat the noun as separate words.

> *Examples*   *eyewitness, eye shadow, eye-opener*

> NOTE: All these words had to be looked up in the dictionary to know what to do with them!

<u>Rule 2</u>. Phrases that have both verb, noun, and adjective forms should appear as separate words when used as verbs and as one word when used as nouns or adjectives.

> *Examples*   *The engine will eventually **break down**.* (verb)
>
> *We suffered a **breakdown** in communications.* (noun)
>
> *Please **clean up** your room.* (verb)
>
> *That Superfund site will require specialized **cleanup** procedures.* (adjective)

<u>Rule 3</u>. Compound verbs are either hyphenated or appear as one word. If you do not find the verb in the dictionary, hyphenate it.

> *Examples*   *To **air-condition** the house will be costly.*
>
> *We were notified that management will **downsize** the organization next year.*

<u>Rule 4</u>. Generally, hyphenate between two or more adjectives when they come before a noun and act as a single idea.

> *Examples*   *friendly-looking man*
> compound adjective in front of a noun
>
> *friendly little girl*
> not a compound adjective
>
> *brightly lit room*
> *Brightly* is an adverb describing *lit*, not an adjective.

HYPHENS continued

Rule 5. When adverbs other than *ly* adverbs are used as compound words in front of a noun, hyphenate. When the combination of words is used after the noun, do not hyphenate.

Examples   The **well-known** actress accepted her award.
Well is an adverb followed by another descriptive word.
They combine to form one idea in front of the noun.

The actress who accepted her award was **well known**.
Well known follows the noun it describes, so no hyphen is used.

A **long-anticipated** decision was finally made.

He had his **much-needed** haircut yesterday.

His haircut was **much needed**.

Rule 6. Remember to use a comma, not a hyphen, between two adjectives when you could have used *and* between them.

Examples   I have important, classified documents.

Jennifer received a lovely, fragrant bouquet on Valentine's Day.

Rule 7. Hyphenate all compound numbers from twenty-one through ninety-nine.

Examples   The teacher had thirty-two children in her classroom.

Only twenty of the children were bilingual.

HYPHENS continued

Hyphens with Prefixes

Rule 1. The current trend is to do away with unnecessary hyphens. Therefore, attach most prefixes and suffixes onto root words without a hyphen.

> *Examples*   *noncompliance, copayment, semiconscious, fortyish*
> *Exception*   *bell-like*
>   Avoid three of any one letter in a row.
> *Exception*   *non-civil service position*
>   Use the hyphen with compound words.

Rule 2. Hyphenate prefixes when they come before proper nouns.

> *Example*   *un-American*

Rule 3. Hyphenate prefixes ending in *a* or *i* only when the root word begins with an *a* or *i*.

> *Examples*   *ultra-ambitious*
>   *semi-invalid*

Rule 4. When a prefix ends in one vowel and a root word begins with a different vowel, generally attach them without a hyphen.

> *Examples*   *antiaircraft, proactive*

Rule 5. Double *e*'s and double *o*'s are usually made into one word.

> *Examples*   *preemployment, coordinate*
> *Exceptions*   *de-emphasize, co-owner*

Rule 6. Hyphenate all words beginning with *self* except for *selfish* and *selfless*.

> *Examples*   *self-assured, self-respect, self-addressed*

HYPHENS continued

Rule 7. Use a hyphen with the prefix *ex*.

    Example   *His ex-wife sued for nonsupport.*

Rule 8. Use the hyphen with the prefix *re* only when:

the *re* means *again*
AND
omitting the hyphen would cause confusion with another word.

    Examples   *Will she recover from her illness?*
                    Re does not mean again.

                    I have re-covered the sofa twice.
                    Re does mean *again*
                    AND
                    omitting the hyphen would have caused confusion with another word.

                    The stamps have been reissued.
                    Re means *again* but would not cause confusion with another word.

                    I must re-press the shirt.
                    Re means *again*
                    AND
                    omitting the hyphen would have caused confusion with another word.

DASHES

En Dash

An **en dash**, which is a little longer than a hyphen, is used for periods of time when you might otherwise use *to*.

Examples	*The years 2001 – 2003*	*[This is how the spacing would appear on a PC]*
	January–June	*[On a Mac, use no spaces or only small spaces surrounding the en dash]*

An **en dash** is also used in place of a hyphen when combining open compounds.

Examples	*North Carolina–Virginia border*
	a high school–college conference

With an **en dash**, spacing is dependent on your computer. If you are using a PC, you have no choice but to use spaces in order to form an en dash. If you are forming an en dash using a PC, hit space, hit the hyphen key, and hit space again before typing in the next word/number. If you are using a Mac, press the option key and the hyphen key to form an en dash.

Em Dash

Use an **em dash** sparingly in formal writing. Don't use it just because you are uncertain about correct punctuation. In informal writing, **em dashes** may replace commas, semicolons, colons, and parentheses to indicate added emphasis, an interruption, or an abrupt change of thought.

On a PC, an em dash is made by using ALT + 0151 (hold down the ALT key and type 0151 on the numeric keypad), with no spaces before or after. It looks like this: —
On a Mac, an **em dash** is made by striking Option, Shift, Hyphen.

Examples	*You are the friend—the only friend—who offered to help me.*
	Never have I met such a lovely person—before you.
	I pay the bills—she has all the fun.
	A semicolon would be used here in formal writing.
	I need three items at the store—dog food, vegetarian chili, and cheddar cheese.
	Remember, a colon would be used here in formal writing.
	My agreement with Fiona is clear—she teaches me French and I teach her German.
	Again, a colon would work here in formal writing.
	Please call my agent—Jessica Cohen—about hiring me.
	Parentheses or commas would work just fine here instead of the dashes.
	I wish you would—oh, never mind.
	This shows an abrupt change in thought and warrants a dash.

While there are many more possible uses of the em dash, by not providing additional rules, I am hoping to curb your temptation to employ this convenient but overused punctuation mark.

CAPITALIZATION

Rule 1. Capitalize the first word of a quoted sentence.

Examples   *He said, "Treat her as you would your own daughter."*

"Look out!" she screamed. "You almost ran into my child."

Rule 2. Capitalize a proper noun.

Example   *Golden Gate Bridge*

Rule 3. Capitalize a person's title when it precedes the name. Do not capitalize when the title is acting as a description following the name.

Examples   *Chairperson Petrov*

Ms. Petrov, the chairperson of the company, will address us at noon.

Rule 4. Capitalize when the person's title follows the name on the address or signature line.

Example   *Sincerely,*
Ms. Haines, Chairperson

Rule 5. Capitalize the titles of high-ranking government officials when used with or before their names. Do not capitalize the civil title if it is used instead of the name.

Examples   *The president will address Congress.*

All senators are expected to attend.

The governors, lieutenant governors called for a special task force.

Governor Fortinbrass, Lieutenant Governor Poppins, Attorney General Dalloway, and Senators James and Twain will attend.

Rule 6. Capitalize any title when used as a direct address.

Example   *Will you take my temperature, Doctor?*

CAPITALIZATION continued

Rule 7. Capitalize points of the compass only when they refer to specific regions.

    Examples   *We have had three relatives visit from the South.*

        Go south three blocks and then turn left.

        We live in the southeast section of town.
        Southeast is just an adjective here describing section, so it should not be capitalized.

Rule 8. Capitalize titles of publications except for little words such *as a, an, the, but, as, if, and, or, nor,* when used internally. If these little words begin the title, capitalize them. Capitalize short verb forms such as *Is, Are,* and *Be.*

    Examples   *The Day of the Jackal*
        What Color Is Your Parachute?
        A Tale of Two Cities

Rule 9. Capitalize *federal* or *state* when used as part of an official agency name or in government documents where these terms represent an official name. If they are being used as general terms, you can use lower case letters.

    Examples   *The state has evidence to the contrary.*

        That is a federal offense.

        The State Board of Equalization collects sales taxes.

        We will visit three states during our summer vacation.

        The Federal Bureau of Investigation has been subject to much scrutiny and criticism lately.

        Her business must comply with all county, state, and federal laws.

Rule 10. You may capitalize words such as *department, bureau,* and *office* if you have prepared your text in the following way:

    Example   *The Bureau of Land Management (Bureau) has some jurisdiction over Indian lands. The Bureau is finding its administrative role to be challenging.*

Rule 11. Do not capitalize names of seasons.

    Example   *I love autumn colors and spring flowers.*

CAPITALIZATION continued

<u>Rule 12</u>. Capitalize the first word of a salutation and the first word of a complimentary close.

     Examples   *Dear Ms. Mohamed:*

                          My dear Mr. Sanchez:

                          Very truly yours,

<u>Rule 13</u>. Capitalize words derived from proper nouns.

     Example   *I must take English and math.*
                          English is capitalized because it comes from the proper noun *England* but *math* does not come from *mathland*.

<u>Rule 14</u>. Capitalize the names of specific course titles.

     Example   *I must take history and Algebra 2.*

WRITING NUMBERS

Rule 1. The numbers *one* through *nine* should be spelled out; use figures for numbers 10 and above.

Examples	*I want five copies.*
	I want 10 copies.

Rule 2. With a group of related numbers where one number is above *nine* in a sentence, write the numbers all in figures. Use words if all related numbers are below 10.

Correct	*I asked for 5 pencils, not 50.*
Incorrect	*I asked for five pencils, not 50.*
Correct	*My 10 cats fought with their 2 cats.*
Correct	*My nine cats fought with their two cats.*

Rule 3. If the numbers are unrelated, then you may use both figures and words. Again, *one* through *nine* should be spelled out.

Examples	*I asked for 30 pencils for my five employees.*
	My nine cavities are exceeded in number by my 14 teeth.
	I have 10 toes but only one nose.

Rule 4. Always spell out simple fractions and use hyphens with them.

Examples	*One-half of the pies have been eaten.*
	A two-thirds majority is required for that bill to pass in Congress.

Rule 5. A mixed fraction can be expressed in figures unless it is the first word of a sentence.

Example	*We expect a 5 1/2 percent wage increase.*
	Five and one-half percent was the maximum allowable interest.

Rule 6. The simplest way to express large numbers is best. Be careful to be consistent within a sentence.

Correct	*You can earn from one million to five million dollars.*
Incorrect	*You can earn from one million to $5,000,000.*
Correct	*You can earn from $500 to $5,000,000.*
Incorrect	*You can earn from $500 to $5 million.*
Correct	*You can earn from five hundred to five million dollars.*
Incorrect	*You can earn from $500 to five million dollars.*

Rule 7. Write decimals in figures. Put a zero in front of a decimal unless the decimal itself begins with a zero.

Examples	*The plant grew 0.79 of a foot in one year.*
	The plant grew only .07 of a foot this year because of the drought.

WRITING NUMBERS continued

Rule 8. When writing out large numbers of five or more digits before the decimal point, use a comma where the comma would appear in the figure format. Use the word *and* only where the decimal point appears in the figure format.

> *Examples* $15,768.13 *(Fifteen thousand, seven hundred sixty-eight dollars and thirteen cents)*
> $1054.21 *(One thousand fifty-four dollars and twenty-one cents)*
> **NOTE:** The comma is now commonly omitted in four-digit whole numbers.

Rule 9. The following examples apply when using dates:

> *Examples*   *The meeting is scheduled for June 30.*
> *The meeting is scheduled for the 30th of June.*
> *We have had tricks played on us on April 1.*
> *The 1st of April puts some people on edge.*

Rule 10. When expressing decades, you may spell them out and lowercase them.

> *Example*   *During the eighties and nineties, the United States economy grew.*

Rule 11. If you wish to express decades using incomplete numerals, put an apostrophe before the incomplete numeral but not between the year and the *s*.

> *Correct*   *During the '80s and '90s, the United States economy grew.*
> *Incorrect*   *During the '80's and '90's, the United States economy grew.*

Rule 12. You may also express decades in complete numerals. Again, don't use an apostrophe between the year and the *s*.

> *Example*   *During the 1980s and 1990s, the United States economy grew.*

Rule 13. Normally, spell out the time of day in text even with half and quarter hours. With *o'clock*, the number is always spelled out.

> *Examples*   *She gets up at four thirty before the baby wakes up.*
> *The baby wakes up at five o'clock in the morning.*

Rule 14. Use numerals with the time of day when exact times are being emphasized.

> *Examples*   *Monib's flight leaves at 6:22 a.m.*
> *Please arrive by 12:30 sharp.*

Rule 15. Use *noon* and *midnight* rather than *12:00 a.m.* or *12:00 p.m.*

Rule 16. Hyphenate all compound numbers from *twenty-one* through *ninety-nine*.

> *Example*   *Forty-three people were injured in the train wreck. Twenty-three of them were hospitalized.*

Rule 17. Write out a number if it begins a sentence.

> *Examples*   *Twenty-nine people won an award for helping their communities.*
> *That 29 people won an award for helping their communities was fantastic!*

GRAMMAR PRETEST

Correct each sentence. Answers are on page 88.

1. How quick he runs.

2. Neither DeAndre nor I are to follow.

3. The desk and the chair sits in the corner.

4. Each of us were scheduled to take the test.

5. The coach, not the players, have been ill.

6. There is only four days until Christmas.

7. She is one of the women who works hard.

8. That was Yusuf and me whom you saw.

9. This phone call is for Bill and I.

10. Terrell is the smartest of the two.

11. It was I whom called.

12. It is us clerks who work hard.

13. He took the plate off of the table.

14. None of the neighbors offered his support.

15. They mailed the copies to him and I.

16. Neither of the candidates have spoken.

17. How will you be effected financially if the effect of downsizing means
   you will lose your job?

18. Joan walks slower so her children can keep up with her.

19. Jake is the oldest of the two brothers.

20. May did good on the test she took yesterday.

21. He and she were real close friends.

22. Whomever drove in the carpool lane without any passengers will be fined.

23. Please allow Jenna or myself to assist you.

24. I work with people that judge others by their nationalities and accents.

25. They fought over their father's estate because they felt angrily about the way he had treated them.

26. You look well in that running outfit.

27. Don't feel badly about forgetting my birthday.

28. We saw two puppies at the pound and took home the cutest one.

29. Speak slower please.

30. Samantha will meet us later on.

31. Pollen effects my sinuses and makes me sneeze.

32. I want to lay down for a nap but the phone keeps ringing.

33. The SUV, that landed on its hood after the accident, was traveling at 80 miles per hour.

34. Yesterday, Barry lay my jacket on the hood of the car.

FINDING SUBJECTS AND VERBS QUIZ 1

Underline the subjects once and the verbs twice. Answers on page 89.

1. He depends on her in times of need.

2. Watch your step.

3. The insurance agent gave her sound advice.

4. On the table was her purse.

5. In the newspaper, an interesting article appeared.

6. Look before you leap.

7. Across the road lived her boyfriend.

8. We are forced to inhale and exhale this smog-filled air.

9. In the gutter, I found a shiny new dime.

10. Around every cloud is a silver lining.

11. Every one of the roses bloomed.

FINDING SUBJECTS AND VERBS QUIZ 2

Underline the verbs twice and the subjects once. Answers on page 89.

1. This gorgeous grand piano is tuned to perfection.
2. Every environmental regulation has been undermined by that industry.
3. My gift for walking and talking simultaneously did not go unnoticed.
4. Your red scarf matches your eyes.
5. Every attempt to flatter him failed miserably.
6. Think before you speak and you will be glad for the things you never said.
7. If all is lost, why am I still playing?
8. Jared longed for a pity party after he lost his job.
9. Have you memorized all the chemical symbols on the chart?
10. *Buses* has only one s in the middle of it.
11. Please answer the question without smirking. (you)

SUBJECT AND VERB AGREEMENT QUIZ 1

Underline the verbs twice and the subjects once. If the subjects and verbs do not agree, change the verbs to match the subjects. Answers on page 89.

1. At the end of the story, they was [were] living happily ever after.
2. Al and Eli go to the beach to surf with their friends.
3. When Al and Eli arrive [arrived], they find [found] that their friends has [had] waxed their boards.
4. The group of children from that school has [have] never seen the ocean.
5. If our staff don't [doesn't] quit picking at each other, we will not meet our goals.
6. Either Gary or I are responsible for allocating the funds.
7. Neither she nor they were willing to predict the election results.
8. Nora is one of the candidates who is worthy of my vote.
9. Nora, of all the candidates who is [are] running, is the best.
10. My problem, which is minor in comparison with others, exist [exist] because I dropped out of high school.
11. His dogs, which are kept outside, bark all day long.

12. There's three strawberries left.

13. Here is the reports from yesterday.

14. Some of my goals has yet to be met.

15. All of my goals are being met and surpassed.

16. None of this is your business.

17. None of them is coming home tonight.

18. One third of the city are experiencing a blackout tonight.

19. One third of the people are suffering.

20. When she talks, we listens.

21. Neither the farmer nor the farmworkers is willing to settle the strike.

22. Neither Darren nor Ida are capable of such a crime.

SUBJECT AND VERB AGREEMENT QUIZ 2

Underline the verbs twice and the subjects once. If the subjects and verbs do not agree, change the verbs to match the subjects. Answers on page 90.

1. The teacher or student is going to appear on stage first.

2. The mother duck, along with all her ducklings, swim so gracefully.

3. Each of those dresses is beautiful.

4. The folder, not the letters, were misplaced.

5. Here is the three doughnuts that you wanted.

6. Five hundred dollars are the price that the dealer is asking.

7. Three fourths of the pies have been eaten.

8. The majority of the state is Republican.

9. A golden retriever is one of those dogs that is always faithful.

10. Every one of the dancers is very limber.

11. The original document, as well as subsequent copies, was lost.

12. Neither the ashtray nor the lamp were on the table.

13. Only forty percent of the eligible voters is going to the polls.

14. Almost all of the newspaper are devoted to advertisements.

15. There are maps hanging on the walls.

16. Here is Shanna and Jessie.

17. The anguish of the victims have gone unnoticed.

18. Taxes on interest is still deferrable.

19. Neither he nor I are going.

20. Is it possible that Jose, as well as his family, are missing?

21. Five dollars are all I have to my name.

22. Neither of the lawyers are willing to take the case.

23. Each of the vacation homes are furnished with pots and pans.

PRONOUNS QUIZ 1

Choose the correct pronoun(s) for each sentence. Answers on page 91.

1. She/Her went to the store.
2. It was she/her.
3. We talked to he/him.
4. It is I/me.
5. Talk to they/them before making a decision.
6. Can you go with we/us?
7. Saleha and she/her have quit the team.
8. They asked he/him and I/me to join the staff.
9. That call was for I/me, not he/him.
10. You didn't tell we/us that they/them were here first.
11. I/me wonder what he/him could have said to she/her.
12. A message arrived for he/him and she/her.
13. Tell Imran and she/her that I/me called.
14. I am as willing as he/him to work hard.
15. She invited he/him to be her escort.
16. Erykah called Damjana and I/me as soon as she could.
17. It is they/them.
18. Beverly is more nervous than she/her.
19. It will be we/us who win this election.
20. Kathleen invited Lester and I/me to the movie.
21. This is he/him speaking.

PRONOUNS <u>QUIZ 2</u>

Fix any pronoun errors in the following sentences. Answers on page 91.

1. Meagan said she looked forward to seeing he and I at the airport.

2. Him and me have been good friends since second grade.

3. If you don't mind me asking, why are you so angry?

4. My friend, unlike myself, is very artistic.

5. Please talk to Daniela or myself next time you have a concern.

6. Ask her, not me.

7. It's a strong strain of bacteria causing this infection.

8. None of the doctors have been able to figure out what is wrong with she or I.

9. She is as stubborn as him, but that's no surprise given they are sister and brother.

10. I weigh more than him.

11. I would rather work with Raven than with her.

12. It is us who deserve credit for this company's third quarter profits.

13. Its a shame that some of the profits have been wasted on excessive
   executive compensation packages.

14. Him complaining just made everyone else more frustrated.

15. I and my friend will stop by on our way to the bakery.

16. You can help him or me but probably not both of us.

17. We regret to inform you that you running the red light has resulted in a ticket.

18. My boss and me will pick up where they left off.

19. When the horse kicked it's legs, the rider bounced off and landed in the lake.

20. You're friend told his' friend to tell my friend that their's a party tonight.

21. The argument he gave had it's merits.

WHO, WHOM, WHOEVER, WHOMEVER QUIZ 1

Choose the correct word for each sentence. Answers on page 92.

1. _____ is your closest friend?

2. _____ do you bank with?

3. _____ do you think will win the award?

4. Clare knows _____ the winner is already.

5. Omar will talk about his girlfriend with _____ asks him.

6. Kimiko donates her time to _____ needs it most.

7. Quinton will work on the project with _____ you suggest.

8. _____ was that in the clown costume?

9. Kathy was not sure _____ she was voting for.

10. _____ wins the lottery will become a millionaire.

11. He is the man _____ was employed here.

12. She is the woman _____ we employed last year.

13. Of _____ were you speaking?

14. _____ do you think will do the work best?

15. He is the man _____ we think you mentioned.

16. I will vote for _____ you suggest.

17. _____ shall I ask about this matter?

18. Give the information to _____ requests it.

19. Tonight we shall find out _____ won.

20. _____ runs this show?

WHO, WHOM, WHOEVER, WHOMEVER QUIZ 2
Choose the correct word for each sentence. Answers on page 93.

1. We intend to notify _____ ranks highest on the list.

2. These are the sign language interpreters _____ I feel you should acknowledge.

3. _____ can we trust in a crisis?

4. Ms. Cohen, _____ has a way with words, will be the valedictorian.

5. The person _____ produces the most work will receive a bonus.

6. _____ are you dancing with next?

7. _____ would you say is the best person for this position?

8. The therapist will talk with _____ needs her help.

9. We are not sure _____ set off the alarm.

10. Don't talk with anyone _____ you think might be connected with the competition.

11. _____ had my job before me?

12. It was she _____ they selected for the Cabinet post.

13. Sometimes it is the one _____ does the most work who is the least tired.

14. We plan to hire an assistant _____ is a good proofreader.

15. The prize will be given to _____ writes the best essay.

16. The bookkeeper is the one to _____ the figures should be mailed.

17. Give the recipe for the vegetarian chili to _____ calls for it.

18. _____ did you really want to be there?

19. She is the contestant _____ they sent to us.

20. This vacation spot will refresh _____ seeks refuge here.

WHO, WHOM, THAT, WHICH <u>QUIZ 1</u>

Correct *who, whom, that,* or *which* in the following sentences. Answers on page 93.

1. Ahmed is the skydiver that broke his back last week.

2. That is a problem that can't be solved without a calculator.

3. That is a promise which cannot be broken.

4. The domino theory, that stated that when one country fell to Communism others in the area would likely fall, was used as an argument to continue the Vietnam War.

5. The game which intrigues Gretchen the most is dominoes.

6. Gandhi, who was a role model for nonviolence to millions, was assassinated.

7. The tomatoes which grow in her garden are unlike those you buy in a store.

8. The tomatoes from her garden, which grew larger than those in the grocery store, were sweet and ripe.

9. The baker that baked that bread should win an award.

WHO, WHOM, THAT, WHICH <u>QUIZ 2</u>

Correct *who, whom, that,* or *which* in the following sentences. Answers on page 94.

1. Books have been discovered which address the horrors of the Salem witch trials.

2. That book that was discovered in the basement of the library, will be published next year.

3. That is a book which I have not yet read.

4. The state law which banned logging ancient redwoods was put on the ballot by voter initiative.

5. The campaign to protect ancient redwoods, which began at the grassroots level, has gained the attention of lawmakers at the national level.

6. The wheelchairs in that corner, which are motorized, are helpful to those who live in urban areas.

7. The people that are on my list haven't shown up yet.

8. The couple in the Halloween masks, which are my parents, left the party an hour ago.

9. Officer, he is the one that stole my purse.

ADJECTIVES AND ADVERBS QUIZ 1

Decide whether each word in bold is being used correctly. If not, change it. Answers on page 94.

1. Come **quick** or we will miss our bus.

2. You drive so **slow** that I am afraid someone will hit the car from behind.

3. I have never been **more surer** of anything in my life.

4. Ella was the **best** of the two sisters at gymnastics.

5. You did that somersault so **good**.

6. Rochelle felt **badly** about forgetting Devlin's birthday.

7. This is the **worst** oil spill I have ever seen.

8. The jasmine has bloomed and smells very **sweet**.

9. You look **angrily**. What did I do?

10. She looked **suspiciously** at the man wearing the trench coat.

11. **These** tree looks as though it is infested with beetles.

12. **Those** bushes need to be trimmed.

13. When was the last time you had no allergy symptoms and felt **good**?

14. In the library, you have to be **more quieter then** when you are outside.

15. She felt **good** about getting her puppy from the SPCA.

16. Charlotte has a **more better** approach to solving that problem.

17. Which is the **worst**, a toothache or a headache?

18. She reacted **swift**, which made him feel **badly** about insulting her.

19. The herbs in the salad tasted **bitter**.

20. Sharon fought **bitterly** against her ex-husband for custody of their daughter.

ADJECTIVES AND ADVERBS <u>QUIZ 2</u>
Decide whether each word in bold is being used correctly. If not, change it. Answers on page 95.

1. We are **real** happy to be of service to you and your family.

2. The perfume smells **sweetly**. *Sweet*

3. I feel **bad** about what happened.

4. Of all the holidays, this is the **most** joyful.

5. This wine tastes **dryly** to me.

6. Don't feel too **badly** about what you said.

7. This leotard hugs me **firmly**.

8. Life in the city is exciting, but life in the country is **best**.

9. If you don't speak **clear**, the audience will not understand you.

10. The **sweet** smell of roses has no match.

11. Walk **slow** or you will be sorry.

12. You don't look as though you feel **well** today.

13. You don't look as though you are doing **well** today.

14. My son doesn't feel very **good** today.

15. She was the **most** beautiful of the two.

16. The dentist said, "I will be finished drilling **real** soon."

17. Speak **slower** or you will lose your audience.

18. Juanita said she had better memories of Paris **then** of Rome.

19. If you won't tell me your secret now, **than** when will you tell me?

20. I would rather have hope **than** hold despair.

PROBLEMS WITH PREPOSITIONS <u>QUIZ 1</u>

Correct the following sentences by adding, removing, or changing the prepositions. Answers on page 95.

1. Our ship leaves August 15.

2. I could of danced all night.

3. Where did you get this from?

4. If we split it evenly between the three of us, no one will be unhappy.

5. You can't just walk in the house without knocking.

6. He will be back the tenth.

7. Take your plate off of the table.

8. Cut the pie up into six slices.

9. Like the invitation stated, we'll see you the tenth for our reunion.

PROBLEMS WITH PREPOSITIONS <u>QUIZ 2</u>

Correct the following sentences by adding, removing, or changing the prepositions. Answers on page 95.

1. Tell me where you found this at.

2. Sami will meet him May 18 at the Washington Hotel in downtown Seattle.

3. I should of known he would steal money from my purse.

4. We hiked into the woods and fell off of a log while crossing a creek.

5. That lie is still coming between the two of them.

6. Like I said, I am sorry for the muddy prints her paws left on the carpet.

7. I should of wiped her paws first.

8. The robbery happened just like you said it did.

EFFECT VS. AFFECT <u>QUIZ 1</u>

Make corrections where needed. Answers on page 96.

1. The affect of the antibiotic on her infection was surprising.

2. I did not know that antibiotics could effect people so quickly.

3. Plastic surgery had an effect, not only on her appearance, but on her self-esteem.

4. If the chemotherapy has no affect, should she get surgery for the tumor?

5. When will we know if the chemotherapy has taken effect?

6. Losing her hair from chemotherapy did not effect her as much as her friends had expected.

7. We cannot effect a new policy without the board of directors voting on it first.

8. To be an affective leader, you should know both your strengths as well as your weaknesses.

9. The movie *Winged Migration* had two effects on him: He became an environmental advocate and a bird lover.

10. The net affect of blowing the whistle on her boss was that she was eventually given his position.

11. What was the affect of his promotion?

12. His decision affected everyone here.

13. We had to effect a reduction in costs.

14. The critics greatly effected his thinking.

15. How were you able to affect such radical changes?

16. That book had a major affect on his philosophy.

EFFECT VS. AFFECT <u>QUIZ 2</u>

Make corrections where needed. Answers on page 96.

1. Shelley had to affect great reductions in her expenses.

2. What do you suppose the effect of her resignation will be?

3. The changes had an enormous affect on production.

4. The crisis has greatly affected our lifestyle.

5. They were able to affect an increase in their savings.

6. Roberta has effected many improvements in office procedures.

7. The rainy weather had a bad affect on attendance at the seminar.

8. The new personnel ruling does not affect my status.

9. The new director will reorganize the office and effect a number of

   changes in personnel.

10. What she said had no affect on the boss.

11. I don't know why the cold air affects my skin.

12. I hope to effect improvements in my work.

13. The knowledge I gain from this course will effect my performance.

14. The new schedule will take affect in October.

15. The supervisor effected a reconciliation between Donya and Dayne.

16. The new law goes into affect tomorrow.

LIE VS. LAY QUIZ 1
Make corrections where needed. Answers on page 97.

1. I am dizzy and need to lay down. lie

2. When I got dizzy yesterday, I laid down.

3. My brother lays carpet for a living.

4. Lay the carpet after painting the walls. _lie_

5. We need to lie this baby down for a nap.

6. We will know when we have lain this issue to rest when we no longer

   fight about it.

7. The lions are laying in wait for their prey.

8. The lions have laid in wait for their prey.

9. I laid the blanket over her as she slept.

10. I will lie my head on my pillow shortly.

LIE VS. LAY QUIZ 2

Make corrections where needed. Answers on page 97.

1. Lay down next to me and I will hold you.

2. When my dog is tired, she lays on her back.

3. I think we can lay the groundwork for lasting changes within the organization.

4. I have laid down with a headache every afternoon this week.

5. Henry has lied consistently on the witness stand.

6. Sandra has lain out her plan for reorganization.

7. The preschoolers have lain down after lunch each day.

8. After I took the pill, I had to lay down.

9. I have laid my cards on the table.

10. Lay on this lounge chair and soak up some sun.

EFFECTIVE WRITING QUIZ 1

Rewrite these sentences to make them more effective. Your sentences may be different from the answers given in the book. Answers on page 98.

1. We are no longer able to reconcile; therefore, attorneys will be used to effect the dissolution of our marriage.

2. The weather had adverse impacts on our boat resulting in the necessity to rescue us from the water.

3. The leak in the bottom of the boat was due to poor maintenance on the part of the crew.

4. Our marriage ended in a divorce.

5. The boy was struck in the face by the pie as it flew from the girl's hand.

6. It was not likely that no one would want to claim ownership of the new sports car.

7. There are many ideas that are worth exploring by us at this meeting.

8. Martin could not find time to work, shop, and go for walks with the dogs.

9. Jordan did not believe that Serena had embarrassed him unintentionally.

10. It is a shame that there are so many holidays that go uncelebrated.

11. While singing in the shower, the bar of soap slipped from her hands.

12. Looking back, the dog was following us.

13. Lying on a stretcher, they carried him out.

14. Flying out the window, he grabbed the papers.

15. Stepping off the bus, the shopping center was just ahead.

EFFECTIVE WRITING QUIZ 2

Change the following sentences to make them more effective. Answers on page 99.

1. It is necessary that you not be uninformed about this case.

2. There is ample evidence which indicates that the attorneys for the defense did not provide inadequate counseling to their client.

3. Speaking and to listen well are important elements of communication.

4. To win is the obvious goal, but playing fair is important too.

5. They were charged with assault, robbery, and forging checks.

6. I remember his generosity and that he was considerate.

7. She worked quickly and in an efficient manner.

8. When working with power tools, eyes should be protected.

9. When changing a diaper, a baby should be on his or her back.

10. I have some letters the mail carrier delivered in my purse.

11. We have tuna casserole I made in the refrigerator.

12. Mollie came over while I was playing the piano with a piece of pound cake.

13. While asleep, the flea bit the dog.

14. I tried calling to tell you about that TV show five times.

15. Although very spicy, Dana managed to finish the enchilada.

GRAMMAR MASTERY TEST

Correct the following sentences. Answers on page 100.

1. Some of the desserts was left by the end of the birthday party.

2. The papa bear thought that some of his porridge were missing.

3. Your brilliant excuses almost makes up for your tardiness.

4. Neither Jackson nor Jenna is playing hooky.

5. Neither Jackson nor I are playing hooky.

6. Either of us is capable of winning.

7. All of the class is willing to take part in the prank.

8. One third of the eligible population tend not to vote in national elections.

9. One third of the voters tends not to cast their ballots in national elections.

10. Here's the paper clips you requested.

11. She is one of those doctors who make house calls.

12. Dr. Cresta is one of those professors who does whatever it takes to get his point across to his students.

13. She is the only professor who does what it takes to help her students learn joyfully.

14. Her and him are always fighting.

15. When Toni and him come over, we always have a great time.

16. It is we who must decide whether to tax ourselves or cut spending.

17. Between you and I, this class is a joke.

18. Who do you think you are to give me advice about dating?

19. Who makes up these English rules anyway?

20. Whom do you think should win?

21. Who are you voting for?

22. Whoever has the keys gets to be in the driver's seat.

23. We are willing to work with whoever you recommend.

24. The thoughts that Ted presented at the meeting were so worthwhile.

25. The thoughts that Ted presented, that were about shifting national priorities, were well received.

26. When you do a job so good, you can expect a raise.

27. Bonnie was a good sport about losing the race.

28. Harry smells good. What is the aftershave he is wearing?

29. Lisa did so well on the test that she was allowed to accelerate to the next level.

30. Our puppy is definitely more sweeter than her brother.

31. With triplets, I have to be careful to divide everything equally between them or they will fight.

32. Karen should of known that her cheap umbrella would break in the storm.

33. Sometimes the effects of our generosity may seem minimal, but our good intentions do make a difference.

34. Ben thought he had lain my jacket on that bench.

PUNCTUATION AND CAPITALIZATION <u>PRETEST</u>

Correct any punctuation or capitalization errors in the following sentences. Some sentences need no correction. Answers on page 101.

1. Go West three blocks and turn right.

2. Yes sir, I will do it immediately.

3. "How," I asked, "Can you always be so forgetful"?

4. The woman, who is standing there, is his ex-wife.

5. Although we have a competent staff; bottlenecks do occur.

6. I did not receive the order; therefore, I will not pay my bill.

7. We offer a variety of drinks, for instance, beer.

8. Is that book your's?

9. We have much to do; for example, the carpets need vacuuming.

10. Estimates for the work have been forwarded, and a breakdown of costs has been included.

11. Because of his embezzling the company went bankrupt.

12. A proposal that makes harassment of whales illegal has just passed.

13. You may; of course, call us anytime you wish.

14. Paolo hurried to the depot to meet his aunt, and two cousins.

15. Finish your job, it is imperative that you do.

16. Sofia and Aidan's house was recently painted.

17. "Stop it!" I said, "Don't ever do that again."

18. I would; therefore like to have an explanation for the missing cash.

19. "Would you like to accompany me"? he asked?

20. I have always had a mental block against Math.

21. He is a strong healthy man.

22. To apply for this job you must have previous experience.

23. Marge, the woman with blonde hair will be our speaker this evening.

24. He thought quickly, and then answered the question in complete detail.

25. He asked if he could be excused?

26. It is hailing; not raining.

27. We will grant you immunity, if you decide to cooperate with us.

28. You signed the contract, consequently you must provide us with the raw
materials.

29. I would like; however, to read the fine print first.

30. You are required to bring the following: Sleeping bag, food, and a sewing kit.

31. The three companie's computers were stolen.

32. The womens' department is upstairs and to your left.

33. It hurt it's paw.

34. One of the lawyer's left her briefcase.

35. "What does it take to become a licensed architect," she asked?

36. I can't remember if her birthday falls on a Saturday, Sunday or Monday next year.

37. I need to locate four states on the map; Arkansas, Ohio, Illinois, and Utah.

38. The clergyman, who united the entire congregation, was Unitarian.

39. The email read, "Hi Camille. I haven't heard from you in two weeks."

40. The veterinarian said, "Unless its bleeding and doesn't stop, don't worry about it."

41. To be able to let go of needing to discuss this with her mother anymore, Wendy decided, "This is her karma not mine."

42. You must study hard, to get good grades at a major university.

COMMAS QUIZ 1

Correct any comma errors. Some sentences need no correction. Answers on page 102.

1. I took Angie the one with the freckles to the movie last night.

2. Jeremy, and I, have had our share of arguments.

3. You are I am sure, telling the truth.

4. She left Albany, New York on January 18 of that year.

5. I need sugar, butter, and eggs, from the grocery store.

6. Please Sasha, come home as soon as you can.

7. Although you may be right I cannot take your word for it.

8. We will grant you immunity if you decide to cooperate with us.

9. I am typing a letter and she is talking on the phone.

10. She finished her work, and then took a long lunch.

11. Mae said "Why don't you come up and see me sometime?"

12. You said I could go, didn't you?

13. To apply for this job you must have a social security card.

14. He seems to be such a lonely, quiet man doesn't he?

15. She wore a brightly colored dress.

16. She has a good healthy attitude about her work.

COMMAS QUIZ 2

Correct any comma errors. Some sentences need no correction. Answers on page 102.

1. Girls, who have red hair, are very lucky.

2. He asked where his hat was.

3. They are, one might say, true believers.

4. Cheryl arrived in Denver Colorado, hoping to find a good job.

5. On July 20, 1969 astronauts landed on the moon for the first time.

6. Life, liberty and the pursuit of happiness are three guarantees granted to us by our forefathers.

7. I told you Jesse, never to ask me that question again.

8. I may as well not speak if you refuse to even listen.

9. I am already finished cooking but he has not taken his shower yet.

10. I walked all the way to the bus stop and waited for a bus for over an hour.

11. It is drizzling not pouring.

12. What a delicious, appetizing meal!

13. Dario drove to the airport to meet his wife and children.

14. Yes I can be ready in five minutes.

15. I will not stop you, if you want to leave.

16. Rosie Hernandez Ph.D. will be our guest speaker.

SEMICOLONS AND COLONS <u>QUIZ 1</u>

Correct any punctuation errors in the following sentences. Answers on page 103.

1. You asked for forgiveness, he granted it to you.

2. We ask; therefore, that you keep this matter confidential.

3. The order was requested six weeks ago, therefore I expected the shipment to arrive by now.

4. The American flag has three colors, namely, red, white, and blue.

5. Clothes are often made from synthetic material; for instance, rayon.

6. If you believe in magic, magical things will happen, but if you do not believe in magic, you will discover nothing to be magical.

7. The orchestra, excluding the violin section; was not up to par.

8. I have been to San Francisco, California, Reno, Nevada, and Seattle, Washington.

9. I need a few items at the store; clothespins, a bottle opener, and napkins.

10. I answered the phone; but no one seemed to be on the other end of the line.

11. I wanted a cup of coffee, not a glass of milk.

12. You have won the following prizes: namely, a car, a trip to Hawaii, and a bathrobe.

13. If you can possibly arrange it, please visit us, but if you cannot, let us know.

14. I gave her a lot of money while we were married hence I do not wish to pay her a dime in alimony.

15. We have a variety of desserts, for instance apple pie.

16. I needed only three cards to win, namely the ten of hearts, the jack of diamonds, and the king of hearts.

17. I needed only three cards to win; the ten of hearts, the jack of diamonds, and the king of hearts.

18. I would; therefore, like to have an explanation for the missing cash.

19. Nature lovers will appreciate seeing: whales, sea lions, and pelicans.

20. He has friends from Iowa and Nebraska and Illinois is his home state.

21. We have set this restriction, do your homework before watching television.

SEMICOLONS AND COLONS <u>QUIZ</u> 2

Correct any punctuation errors in the following sentences. Answers on page 104.

1. He has friends from Montana Iowa and Nebraska and Illinois is his home state.

2. This is a difficult exercise but I am having fun.

3. Although this is a difficult exercise I am having fun.

4. This is a difficult exercise I am having fun though.

5. The man who is wearing dark glasses is an FBI undercover agent.

6. That FBI agent who is wearing dark glasses once protected the President.

7. Did you John eat my cake?

8. Did John eat my cake?

9. Did his friend John eat my cake?

10. Did John his friend eat the cake?

11. If everything goes according to plan he will retire at 40 if real estate prices continue to drop however he may have to work until he is 65.

12. Golden retrievers, which are known to be gentle are also loyal.

13. Dogs that are gentle are often good family pets.

14. I would love to be rich and famous although fame has mixed blessings.

15. I would love to be rich and famous and famous is the first priority.

16. She chose the field of journalism because of Nellie Bly the first woman reporter.

17. They built an adobe house but then they decided to move.

18. They built an adobe house but then decided to move.

19. They built an adobe house however they decided to move.

20. They built an adobe house because they decided never to move again.

21. Since they moved to the desert they decided to build an adobe house.

22. Mr. Liu held this belief, if he worked hard, he would be able to save enough money to travel to Madagascar and photograph rarely seen animals.

QUESTION MARKS, QUOTATION MARKS, AND PARENTHESES QUIZ 1

Correct any errors in the following sentences. Answers on page 104.

1. He wanted to know when you will be here?

2. "Well, she said, "you certainly didn't waste any time."

3. "Is it almost over?" he asked?

4. "I've had it up to here!", she screamed.

5. The song asks, "Would you like to swing on a star"?

6. Carmen said, "She said, "I'll never leave you."

7. She requested (actually she pleaded, that her name be withheld.

8. This contract guarantees that we will 1 deliver the merchandise, 2 pay for all damaged goods, and 3 make you the exclusive carrier of our products.

9. "May I have a rain check on that lunch"? I asked.

10. Do you believe the saying, "It is better to vote for what you want and not get it than to vote for what you don't want and get it?"

QUESTION MARKS, QUOTATION MARKS, AND PARENTHESES QUIZ 2

Correct any errors in the following sentences. Answers on page 105.

1. "Correct me if I am wrong." She said.

2. "Correct me if I am wrong" she said, "but don't you usually drive a truck?"

3. Sandi asked, "Did Jeri say, 'I am pregnant?'"

4. I can have lunch with you tomorrow (Friday.)

5. I hope you are feeling better (I am sick today.)

6. Did he ask? "Where are my keys"?

7. Harry needs to know if he can count on you?

8. I smiled (actually I laughed) when I saw the expression on his face.

9. Nicole said with shock in her voice! "I can't believe what I just saw."

APOSTROPHES QUIZ 1

Correct any apostrophe errors. Answers on page 105.

1. Her husbands wallet was full of curious, little items.

2. I went to my mother-in-law house for dinner last night.

3. You may not enter Mr. Harris office without his permission.

4. The girls vitality and humor were infectious. (one girl)

5. The womens dresses are on the second floor.

6. Its a shame that had to happen.

7. Its hard to believe that winter is almost here.

8. Her mother and father business went bankrupt.

9. It is his' word against mine.

10. The actresses costumes looked beautiful on them.

11. Sharon arriving was unexpected.

12. The movie had it's desired effect.

APOSTROPHES QUIZ 2

Correct any apostrophe errors. Answers on page 106.

1. His 6's and 8's looked alike.

2. Where would I find the mens room?

3. Both secretary vacations caused a delay in output.

4. New clients accounts showed an 11 percent increase in sales.

    (clients is plural)

5. Most children imaginations run wild when told that story.

6. Both son-in-law opinions were considered.

7. Several M.D. agreed that one bacterial strain caused many of the symptoms.

8. These M.D. credentials are excellent.

9. Both brother-in-law jobs required physical labor.

10. Do you mind me looking at the earrings in this jewelry case?

11. You're right to privacy will not be abused.

12. It's beauty is unsurpassed.

HYPHENS QUIZ 1
Correct the following sentences. Answers on page 106.

1. She jumped from a two story building.

2. The show's cancellation was a real letdown.

3. You must let-down your guard.

4. You certainly have a go get it nature.

5. What a cute little bird she has!

6. We offer around the clock coverage.

HYPHENS QUIZ 2
Correct the following sentences. Answers on page 106.

1. Turn left after the big red door.

2. This is a one family dwelling.

3. Do you think he has above average intelligence?

4. I would like that antique picture frame.

5. She owns income producing property.

6. That is a well written letter.

HYPHENS WITH ly WORDS QUIZ 1
Insert hyphens where appropriate in the following sentences. Answers on page 106.

1. This appears to be a firmly built house.

2. A dimly lit restaurant can be rather romantic.

3. A friendly little dog is all I need for company.

4. The data was readily available.

5. He is a happily married man.

6. What kindly looking eyes my grandfather had.

HYPHENS WITH ly WORDS QUIZ 2

Insert hyphens where appropriate in the following sentences. Answers on page 107.

1. You are certainly a likely looking prospect for the job.

2. A silly acting child is a joy to behold.

3. A chilly snowy morning would be a refreshing sight.

4. The lovely sounding music came from that singer over there.

5. The friendly acting dog growled whenever he had a bone nearby.

6. She appears to be happily married.

HYPHENS WITH PREFIXES QUIZ 1

Insert hyphens where appropriate. Answers on page 107.

1. anti aircraft

2. ultra anxious

3. anti depressant

4. anti freeze

5. anti impressionism

6. un patriotic

7. non professional

8. non existent

HYPHENS WITH PREFIXES QUIZ 2

Insert hyphens where appropriate. Answers on page 107.

1. non Jewish

2. pre existing

3. re establish

4. self satisfied

5. ex Marine

6. anti inflammatory

7. anti war

8. un natural

HYPHENS WITH re WORDS QUIZ 1

Insert hyphens where appropriate. Answers on page 107.

1. When can we re furnish our home?

2. Our friendship was re newed.

3. I cannot re collect the story.

4. Please re collect the papers, Mikaela.

5. That point should be re emphasized.

6. I enjoy re covering chairs.

HYPHENS WITH re WORDS QUIZ 2

Insert hyphens where appropriate. Answers on page 108.

1. The astronauts began the re entry phase.

2. Martin Luther began the Re formation.

3. I made a mistake and had to re form the clay.

4. I must re press the wrinkled suit.

5. I will re lease the apartment after the current tenants leave. (lease again)

6. The couple was re united after a long separation.

CAPITALIZATION QUIZ 1

Correct the following sentences if an error appears. Answers on page 108.

1. She said, "bees are not the only insects that sting."

2. "You must understand," he pleaded, "That I need more time to pay you."

3. Mark Paxton, the Vice President of the company, embezzled over one million dollars.

4. The President of the United States wields much power.

5. I live in the northeastern part of the state where the climate is colder.

6. The West, especially California, is famous for its cutting-edge technology.

7. Have you read *All The King's Men*?

8. I enjoy Summer more than any other season.

9. Employees of the Company were laid off with little hope of returning to work.

10. My Dear Mr. Simpson:

11. Sincerely Yours,

CAPITALIZATION QUIZ 2

Correct the following sentences if an error appears. Answers on page 108.

1. I lived on Elm street a few years ago.

2. The American river is extremely cold all year.

3. Do not swim in that River because of the swift current.

4. "You must realize," he explained, "that my circumstances are desperate."

5. "Stop it!" she screamed. "don't ever do that again."

6. She said, "we strive hard for a better world, but we don't lift a finger for perfection."

7. The west has a milder climate than the east.

8. You must take the following courses: history, geometry, and french.

9. The supervisor will decide whether state regulations prohibit our taking Monday as a holiday.

10. My major requires that I take Calculus 1, History, and French.

11. The federal reserve board will raise interest rates over many State agencies' objections.

PUNCTUATION AND CAPITALIZATION <u>MASTERY TEST</u>

Correct any punctuation or capitalization errors in the following sentences. Some sentences need no correction. Answers on page 109.

1. I am asking if you would like to rollerblade together tomorrow?

2. Yes Jean, you were right about that answer.

3. I read in a book, "If all else fails, succeed; if all else succeeds . . ."

4. Wherever we go people recognize us.

5. Whenever Cheryl is in town she visits her sister.

6. Isabel enjoys the museum although she cannot afford the entrance fee.

7. It may not be the correct part but I bet that it works.

8. You are my friend, however, I cannot afford to lend you any more money.

9. Paul Simon sang, "I am a rock, I am an island."

10. At graduation, the principal said, "I believe that all of you are capable

    of greatness . . . All of you have studied everything you need to succeed."

    (Two separate sentences with a missing sentence between them)

11. I asked Ella, "Did he ask for his ring back"?

12. John F. Kennedy, Jr. became a magazine publisher and a pilot before his

    tragic death.

13. Please contact me if you have any questions.

14. The elections will be held on the first Tuesday of November 2008.

15. The elections, will be held on Tuesday, November 4, 2008, and the polls

    will be kept open until 8:00 p.m.

16. Carl worried about the hurricane but tried to stay calm and help his family.

17. I favor green and yellow and purple is her first choice.

18. I need to locate four states on the map: namely, Minnesota, Michigan,

    California, and Nevada.

19. This is the point that Einstein made; You cannot fix a problem with the

    problem.

20. Our philosophy teacher thinks that Einstein meant that we cannot stop war by waging war.

21. A well made argument was presented for negotiating a peaceful resolution.

22. The argument for negotiating a peaceful resolution was well made.

23. A liberally sprinkled dose of humor was very much appreciated.

24. Our liberal minded clergyman managed to unite the entire congregation.

25. Our clergyman, who united the entire congregation, was liberal-minded.

26. Jan asked, "What did Joe mean when he said, 'I will see you later?'"

27. When I noticed that our dog cut it's paw, I called the veterinarian right away.

28. Just to be sure, I called three more D.V.M.'s offices.

29. "Your right to be concerned," said one veterinarian. "I would like to take a look at your dog."

30. Even though its 30 miles to the town where that D.V.M.'s office is, I wanted to take the drive.

31. The friendly looking vet examined our dog's paw and suggested we have it bandaged.

32. We had pet insurance but still owed $40 in copayment fees.

33. Our dog was a semi-invalid for a couple of days until she chewed off the bandage.

34. I guess she did what any self respecting dog would do by grooming herself.

35. The dog has fully re-covered although I will never be the same.

36. I have learned that it's better to be pro-active than to have regrets.

37. Wendy thought she knew everything about her mother but found out two years ago that her mother had been married before.

38. When Wendy asked her mother about this marriage, Ilse (her mother) was hesitant to discuss any details.

39. She will go to her grave with some secrets thought Wendy.

40. "Do you understand her need for privacy," Wendy asked her husband?

GRAMMAR PRETEST ANSWERS

1. How quickly he runs.
2. Neither DeAndre nor I am to follow.
3. The desk and the chair sit in the corner.
4. Each of us was scheduled to take the test.
5. The coach, not the players, has been ill.
6. There are only four days until Christmas.
7. She is one of the women who work hard.
8. That was Yusuf and I whom you saw.
9. This phone call is for Bill and me.
10. Terrell is the smarter of the two.
11. It was I who called.
12. It is we clerks who work hard.
13. He took the plate off the table.
14. None of the neighbors offered their support.
15. They mailed the copies to him and me.
16. Neither of the candidates has spoken.
17. How will you be affected financially if the effect of downsizing means you will lose your job?
18. Joan walks slowly so her children can keep up with her. (**OR** *more slowly*)
19. Jake is the older of the two brothers.
20. May did well on the test she took yesterday.
21. He and she were really close friends. (**OR** *very*)
22. Whoever drove in the carpool lane without any passengers will be fined.
23. Please allow Jenna or me to assist you.
24. I work with people who judge others by their nationalities and accents.
25. They fought over their father's estate because they felt angry about the way he had treated them.
26. You look good in that running outfit.
27. Don't feel bad about forgetting my birthday.
28. We saw two puppies at the pound and took home the cuter one.
29. Speak more slowly please.
30. Samantha will meet us later.
31. Pollen affects my sinuses and makes me sneeze.
32. I want to lie down for a nap but the phone keeps ringing.
33. The SUV, which landed on its hood after the accident, was traveling at 80 miles per hour.
34. Yesterday, Barry laid my jacket on the hood of the car.

FINDING SUBJECTS AND VERBS <u>QUIZ 1 ANSWERS</u>

1. <u>He</u> <u>depends</u> on her in times of need.
2. (<u>You</u>)<u>Watch</u> your step.
3. The insurance <u>agent</u> <u>gave</u> her sound advice.
4. On the table <u>was</u> her <u>purse</u>.
5. In the newspaper, an interesting <u>article</u> <u>appeared</u>.
6. (<u>You</u>) <u>Look</u> before <u>you</u> <u>leap</u>.
7. Across the road <u>lived</u> her <u>boyfriend</u>.
8. <u>We</u> <u>are forced</u> to inhale and exhale this smog-filled air.
9. In the gutter, <u>I</u> <u>found</u> a shiny new dime.
10. Around every cloud <u>is</u> a silver <u>lining</u>.
11. Every <u>one</u> of the roses <u>bloomed</u>.

FINDING SUBJECTS AND VERBS <u>QUIZ 2 ANSWERS</u>

1. This gorgeous grand <u>piano</u> <u>is tuned</u> to perfection.
2. Every environmental <u>regulation</u> <u>has been undermined</u> by that industry.
3. My <u>gift</u> for walking and talking simultaneously <u>did</u> not <u>go</u> unnoticed.
4. Your red <u>scarf</u> <u>matches</u> your eyes.
5. Every <u>attempt</u> to flatter him <u>failed</u> miserably.
6. (<u>You</u>) <u>Think</u> before <u>you</u> <u>speak</u> and <u>you</u> <u>will be</u> glad for the things <u>you</u> never <u>said</u>.
7. If <u>all</u> <u>is</u> lost, why <u>am</u> <u>I</u> still <u>playing</u>?
8. <u>Jared</u> <u>longed</u> for a pity party after <u>he</u> <u>lost</u> his job.
9. <u>Have</u> <u>you</u> <u>memorized</u> all the chemical symbols on the chart?
10. *<u>Buses</u>* <u>has</u> only one *s* in the middle of it.
11. (<u>You</u>) Please <u>answer</u> the question without smirking.

SUBJECT AND VERB AGREEMENT <u>QUIZ 1 ANSWERS</u>

1. At the end of the story, <u>they</u> <u>were living</u> happily ever after.
2. <u>Al</u> and <u>Eli</u> <u>go</u> to the beach to surf with their friends. (CORRECT)
3. When <u>Al</u> and <u>Eli</u> <u>arrive</u>, <u>they</u> <u>find</u> that their <u>friends</u> <u>have waxed</u> their boards.
4. The <u>group</u> of children from that school <u>has</u> never <u>seen</u> the ocean. (CORRECT)
5. If our <u>staff</u> <u>don't quit</u> picking at each other, <u>we</u> <u>will</u> not <u>meet</u> our goals.
    (CORRECT **OR** If our staff <u>members</u> <u>don't quit</u> picking…)
6. Either <u>Gary</u> or <u>I</u> <u>am</u> responsible for allocating the funds.
7. Neither <u>she</u> nor <u>they</u> <u>were willing</u> to predict the election results. (CORRECT)
8. <u>Nora</u> <u>is</u> one of the candidates <u>who</u> <u>are</u> worthy of my vote.
9. <u>Nora</u>, of all the candidates <u>who</u> <u>are</u> running, <u>is</u> the best.
10. My <u>problem</u>, <u>which</u> <u>is</u> minor in comparison with others, <u>exists</u> because <u>I</u> <u>dropped out</u> of high school.
11. His <u>dogs</u>, <u>which</u> <u>are kept</u> outside, <u>bark</u> all day long. (CORRECT)

12. There <u>are</u> three <u>strawberries</u> left.

13. Here <u>are</u> the <u>reports</u> from yesterday.

14. <u>Some</u> of my goals <u>have</u> yet to be met.

15. <u>All</u> of my goals <u>are being met</u> and <u>surpassed</u>. (CORRECT)

16. <u>None</u> of this <u>is</u> your business.(CORRECT)

17. <u>None</u> of them <u>are coming</u> home tonight.

18. <u>One third</u> of the city <u>is experiencing</u> a blackout tonight.

19. <u>One third</u> of the people <u>are suffering.</u> (CORRECT)

20. When <u>she</u> <u>talks</u>, <u>we</u> <u>listen</u>.

21. Neither the <u>farmer</u> nor the <u>farmworkers</u> <u>are willing</u> to settle the strike.

22. Neither <u>Darren</u> nor <u>Ida</u> <u>is</u> capable of such a crime.

SUBJECT AND VERB AGREEMENT QUIZ 2 ANSWERS

1. The <u>teacher</u> or <u>student</u> <u>is going</u> to appear on stage first.(CORRECT)

2. The mother <u>duck</u>, along with all her ducklings, <u>swims</u> so gracefully.

3. <u>Each</u> of those dresses <u>is</u> beautiful. (CORRECT)

4. The <u>folder</u>, not the letters, <u>was misplaced</u>.

5. Here <u>are</u> the three <u>doughnuts</u> that <u>you</u> <u>wanted</u>.

6. <u>Five hundred dollars</u> <u>is</u> the price that the <u>dealer</u> <u>is asking</u>.

7. <u>Three fourths</u> of the pies <u>have been eaten</u>. (CORRECT)

8. The <u>majority</u> of the state <u>is</u> Republican. (CORRECT)

9. A <u>golden retriever</u> <u>is</u> one of those dogs <u>that</u> <u>are</u> always faithful.

10. Every <u>one</u> of the dancers <u>is</u> very limber. (CORRECT)

11. The original <u>document</u>, as well as subsequent copies, <u>was</u> lost. (CORRECT)

12. Neither the <u>ashtray</u> nor the <u>lamp</u> <u>was</u> on the table.

13. Only <u>forty percent</u> of the eligible voters <u>are</u> going to the polls.

14. Almost <u>all</u> of the newspaper <u>is</u> devoted to advertisements.

15. There <u>are</u> maps <u>hanging</u> on the walls. (CORRECT)

16. Here <u>are</u> <u>Shanna</u> and <u>Jessie</u>.

17. The <u>anguish</u> of the victims <u>has</u> gone unnoticed.

18. <u>Taxes</u> on interest <u>are</u> still deferrable.

19. Neither <u>he</u> nor <u>I</u> <u>am</u> <u>going</u>.

20. <u>Is</u> <u>it</u> possible that <u>Jose</u>, as well as his family, <u>is</u> missing?

21. <u>Five dollars</u> <u>is</u> all <u>I</u> <u>have</u> to my name.

22. <u>Neither</u> of the lawyers <u>is</u> willing to take the case.

23. <u>Each</u> of the vacation homes <u>is</u> furnished with pots and pans.

PRONOUNS QUIZ 1 ANSWERS

1. She went to the store.
2. It was she. (This is preferred although using *her* is considered acceptable by some English teachers.)
3. We talked to him.
4. It is I. (Preferred over *me.*)
5. Talk to them before making a decision.
6. Can you go with us?
7. Saleha and she have quit the team.
8. They asked him and me to join the staff.
9. That call was for me, not him.
10. You didn't tell us that they were here first.
11. I wonder what he could have said to her.
12. A message arrived for him and her.
13. Tell Imran and her that I called.
14. I am as willing as he to work hard.
15. She invited him to be her escort.
16. Erykah called Damjana and me as soon as she could.
17. It is they. (Preferred over *them.*)
18. Beverly is more nervous than she.
19. It will be we who win this election. (Preferred over *us.*)
20. Kathleen invited Lester and me to the movie.
21. This is he speaking. (Preferred over *him.*)

PRONOUNS QUIZ 2 ANSWERS

1. Meagan said she looked forward to seeing **him** and **me** at the airport.
2. **He** and **I** have been good friends since second grade.
3. If you don't mind **my** asking, why are you so angry?
4. My friend, unlike **me**, is very artistic.
5. Please talk to Daniela or **me** next time you have a concern.
6. Ask her, not me. (CORRECT)
7. It's a strong strain of bacteria causing this infection. (CORRECT)
8. None of the doctors have been able to figure out what is wrong with **her** or **me**.
9. She is as stubborn as **he**, but that's no surprise given they are sister and brother.
10. I weigh more than **he**.
11. I would rather work with Raven than with her. (CORRECT)
12. It is **we** who deserve credit for this company's third quarter profits. (Preferred over *us.*)

13. **It's** a shame that some of the profits have been wasted on excessive executive compensation packages.

14. **His** complaining just made everyone else more frustrated.

15. **My friend** and **I** will stop by on our way to the bakery.

16. You can help him or me but probably not both of us. (CORRECT)

17. We regret to inform you that **your** running the red light has resulted in a ticket.

18. My boss and **I** will pick up where they left off.

19. When the horse kicked **its** legs, the rider bounced off and landed in the lake.

20. **Your** friend told **his** friend to tell my friend that **there's** (**OR** there is) a party tonight.

21. The argument he gave had **its** merits.

WHO, WHOM, WHOEVER, WHOMEVER <u>QUIZ 1 ANSWERS</u>

1. Who is your closest friend?

2. Whom do you bank with? **OR** With whom do you bank?

3. Who do you think will win the award?

4. Clare knows who the winner is already.

5. Omar will talk about his girlfriend with whoever asks him.

6. Kimiko donates her time to whoever needs it most.

7. Quinton will work on the project with whomever you suggest.

8. Who was that in the clown costume?

9. Kathy was not sure whom she was voting for.

10. Whoever wins the lottery will become a millionaire.

11. He is the man who was employed here.

12. She is the woman whom we employed last year.

13. Of whom were you speaking?

14. Who do you think will do the work best?

15. He is the man whom we think you mentioned.

16. I will vote for whomever you suggest.

17. Whom shall I ask about this matter?

18. Give the information to whoever requests it.

19. Tonight we shall find out who won.

20. Who runs this show?

WHO, WHOM, WHOEVER, WHOMEVER <u>QUIZ 2 ANSWERS</u>

1. We intend to notify whoever ranks highest on the list.
2. These are the sign language interpreters whom I feel you should acknowledge.
3. Whom can we trust in a crisis?
4. Ms. Cohen, who has a way with words, will be the valedictorian.
5. The person who produces the most work will receive a bonus.
6. Whom are you dancing with next?
7. Who would you say is the best person for this position?
8. The therapist will talk with whoever needs her help.
9. We are not sure who set off the alarm.
10. Don't talk with anyone who you think might be connected with the competition.
11. Who had my job before me?
12. It was she whom they selected for the Cabinet post.
13. Sometimes it is the one who does the most work who is the least tired.
14. We plan to hire an assistant who is a good proofreader.
15. The prize will be given to whoever writes the best essay.
16. The bookkeeper is the one to whom the figures should be mailed.
17. Give the recipe for the vegetarian chili to whoever calls for it.
18. Whom did you really want to be there?
19. She is the contestant whom they sent to us.
20. This vacation spot will refresh whoever seeks refuge here.

WHO, WHOM, THAT, WHICH <u>QUIZ 1 ANSWERS</u>

1. Ahmed is the skydiver **who** broke his back last week.
2. That is a problem **which** can't be solved without a calculator.
3. That is a promise **which** cannot be broken. (CORRECT)
4. The domino theory, **which** stated that when one country fell to Communism others in the area would likely fall, was used as an argument to continue the Vietnam War.
5. The game **that** intrigues Gretchen the most is dominoes.
6. Gandhi, **who** was a role model for nonviolence to millions, was assassinated. (CORRECT)
7. The tomatoes **that** grow in her garden are unlike those you buy in a store.
8. The tomatoes from her garden, **which** grew larger than those in the grocery store, were sweet and ripe. (CORRECT)
9. The baker **who** baked that bread should win an award.

WHO, WHOM, THAT, WHICH <u>QUIZ 2 ANSWERS</u>

1. Books have been discovered **that** address the horrors of the Salem witch trials.
2. That book, **which** was discovered in the basement of the library, will be published next year.
3. That is a book **which** I have not yet read. (CORRECT)
4. The state law **that** banned logging ancient redwoods was put on the ballot by voter initiative.
5. The campaign to protect ancient redwoods, **which** began at the grassroots level, has gained the attention of lawmakers at the national level. (CORRECT)
6. The wheelchairs in that corner, **which** are motorized, are helpful to those who live in urban areas. (CORRECT)
7. The people **who** are on my list haven't shown up yet.
8. The couple in the Halloween masks, **who** are my parents, left the party an hour ago.
9. Officer, he is the one **who** stole my purse.

ADJECTIVES AND ADVERBS <u>QUIZ 1 ANSWERS</u>

1. Come **quickly** or we will miss our bus.
2. You drive so **slowly** that I am afraid someone will hit the car from behind.
3. I have never been **more sure** of anything in my life. (**OR** surer)
4. Ella was the **better** of the two sisters at gymnastics.
5. You did that somersault so **well**.
6. Rochelle felt **bad** about forgetting Devlin's birthday.
7. This is the **worst** oil spill I have ever seen. (CORRECT)
8. The jasmine has bloomed and smells very **sweet**. (CORRECT)
9. You look **angry**. What did I do?
10. She looked **suspiciously** at the man wearing the trench coat. (CORRECT)
11. **This** tree looks as though it is infested with beetles.
12. **Those** bushes need to be trimmed. (CORRECT)
13. When was the last time you had no allergy symptoms and felt **well**?
14. In the library, you have to be **quieter than** when you are outside.
15. She felt **good** about getting her puppy from the SPCA. (CORRECT)
16. Charlotte has a **better** approach to solving that problem.
17. Which is **worse**, a toothache or a headache?
18. She reacted **swiftly**, which made him feel **bad** about insulting her.
19. The herbs in the salad tasted **bitter**. (CORRECT)
20. Sharon fought **bitterly** against her ex-husband for custody of their daughter. (CORRECT)

ADJECTIVES AND ADVERBS <u>QUIZ 2 ANSWERS</u>

1. We are **really** happy to be of service to you and your family. (**OR** very)
2. The perfume smells **sweet**.
3. I feel **bad** about what happened. (CORRECT)
4. Of all the holidays, this is the **most** joyful. (CORRECT)
5. This wine tastes **dry** to me.
6. Don't feel too **bad** about what you said.
7. This leotard hugs me **firmly**. (CORRECT)
8. Life in the city is exciting, but life in the country is **better**.
9. If you don't speak **clearly**, the audience will not understand you.
10. The **sweet** smell of roses has no match. (CORRECT)
11. Walk **slowly** or you will be sorry.
12. You don't look as though you feel **well** today. (CORRECT)
13. You don't look as though you are doing **well** today. (CORRECT)
14. My son doesn't feel very **well** today.
15. She was the **more** beautiful of the two.
16. The dentist said, "I will be finished drilling **really** soon." (**OR** *very*)
17. Speak **slowly** or you will lose your audience. (**OR** *more slowly*)
18. Juanita said she had better memories of Paris **than** of Rome.
19. If you won't tell me your secret now, **then** when will you tell me?
20. I would rather have hope **than** hold despair. (CORRECT)

PROBLEMS WITH PREPOSITIONS <u>QUIZ 1 ANSWERS</u>

1. Our ship leaves **on** August 15.
2. I could **have** danced all night.
3. Where did you get this?
4. If we split it evenly **among** the three of us, no one will be unhappy.
5. You can't just walk **into** the house without knocking.
6. He will be back **on** the tenth.
7. Take your plate off the table.
8. Cut the pie into six slices.
9. **As** the invitation stated, we'll see you **on** the tenth for our reunion.

PROBLEMS WITH PREPOSITIONS <u>QUIZ 2 ANSWERS</u>

1. Tell me where you found this.
2. Sami will meet him **on** May 18 at the Washington Hotel in downtown Seattle.
3. I should **have** known he would steal money from my purse.
4. We hiked into the woods and fell off a log while crossing a creek.
5. That lie is still coming between the two of them. (CORRECT)
6. **As** I said, I am sorry for the muddy prints her paws left on the carpet.
7. I should **have** wiped her paws first.
8. The robbery happened just **as** you said it did.

EFFECT VS. AFFECT QUIZ 1 ANSWERS

1. The effect of the antibiotic on her infection was surprising.

2. I did not know that antibiotics could affect people so quickly.

3. Plastic surgery had an effect, not only on her appearance, but on her self-esteem. (CORRECT)

4. If the chemotherapy has no effect, should she get surgery for the tumor?

5. When will we know if the chemotherapy has taken effect? (CORRECT)

6. Losing her hair from chemotherapy did not affect her as much as her friends had expected.

7. We cannot effect a new policy without the board of directors voting on it first. (CORRECT)

8. To be an effective leader, you should know both your strengths as well as your weaknesses.

9. The movie *Winged Migration* had two effects on him: He became an environmental advocate and a bird lover. (CORRECT)

10. The net effect of blowing the whistle on her boss was that she was eventually given his position.

11. What was the effect of his promotion?

12. His decision affected everyone here. (CORRECT)

13. We had to effect a reduction in costs. (CORRECT)

14. The critics greatly affected his thinking.

15. How were you able to effect such radical changes?

16. That book had a major effect on his philosophy.

EFFECT VS. AFFECT QUIZ 2 ANSWERS

1. Shelley had to effect great reductions in her expenses.

2. What do you suppose the effect of her resignation will be? (CORRECT)

3. The changes had an enormous effect on production.

4. The crisis has greatly affected our lifestyle. (CORRECT)

5. They were able to effect an increase in their savings.

6. Roberta has effected many improvements in office procedures. (CORRECT)

7. The rainy weather had a bad effect on attendance at the seminar.

8. The new personnel ruling does not affect my status. (CORRECT)

9. The new director will reorganize the office and effect a number of changes in personnel. (CORRECT)

10. What she said had no effect on the boss.

11. I don't know why the cold air affects my skin. (CORRECT)

12. I hope to effect improvements in my work. (CORRECT)

13. The knowledge I gain from this course will affect my performance.

14. The new schedule will take effect in October.

15. The supervisor effected a reconciliation between Donya and Dayne. (CORRECT)

16. The new law goes into effect tomorrow.

LIE VS. LAY **QUIZ 1 ANSWERS**

1. I am dizzy and need to **lie** down.
2. When I got dizzy yesterday, I **lay** down.
3. My brother **lays** carpet for a living. (CORRECT)
4. **Lay** the carpet after painting the walls. (CORRECT)
5. We need to **lay** this baby down for a nap.
6. We will know when we have **laid** this issue to rest when we no longer fight about it.
7. The lions are **lying** in wait for their prey.
8. The lions have **lain** in wait for their prey.
9. I **laid** the blanket over her as she slept. (CORRECT)
10. I will **lay** my head on my pillow shortly.

LIE VS. LAY **QUIZ 2 ANSWERS**

1. **Lie** down next to me and I will hold you.
2. When my dog is tired, she **lies** on her back.
3. I think we can **lay** the groundwork for lasting changes within the organization. (CORRECT)
4. I have **lain** down with a headache every afternoon this week.
5. Henry has **lied** consistently on the witness stand. (CORRECT)
6. Sandra has **laid** out her plan for reorganization.
7. The preschoolers have **lain** down after lunch each day. (CORRECT)
8. After I took the pill, I had to **lie** down.
9. I have **laid** my cards on the table. (CORRECT)
10. **Lie** on this lounge chair and soak up some sun.

EFFECTIVE WRITING QUIZ 1 ANSWERS

1. We are no longer able to reconcile; therefore, attorneys will be used to effect the dissolution of our marriage.

   We have hired attorneys to help us with our divorce.

2. The weather had adverse impacts on our boat resulting in the necessity to rescue us from the water.

   Our boat capsized in the storm so we needed rescuing.

3. The leak in the bottom of the boat was due to poor maintenance on the part of the crew.

   The crew did not maintain the boat so the bottom leaked.

4. Our marriage ended in a divorce.

   We divorced. **OR** *We ended our marriage.*

5. The boy was struck in the face by the pie as it flew from the girl's hand.

   The girl threw the pie and it hit the boy's face.

6. It was not likely that no one would want to claim ownership of the new sports car.

   Someone will most likely want to claim ownership of the new sports car.

7. There are many ideas that are worth exploring by us at this meeting.

   Let's explore the many worthwhile ideas at this meeting.

8. Martin could not find time to work, shop, and go for walks with the dogs.

   Martin could not find time to work, shop, and walk the dogs.

9. Jordan did not believe that Serena had embarrassed him unintentionally.

   Jordan believed that Serena had embarrassed him intentionally.

10. It is a shame that there are so many holidays that go uncelebrated.

    It is a shame that so many holidays go uncelebrated. **OR**

    I wish we celebrated more holidays.

11. While singing in the shower, the bar of soap slipped from her hands.

    The bar of soap slipped from her hands while she sang in the shower.

12. Looking back, the dog was following us.

    When we looked back, we saw the dog following us.

13. Lying on a stretcher, they carried him out.

    He was carried out on a stretcher.

14. Flying out the window, he grabbed the papers.

    He grabbed the papers as they flew out the window.

15. Stepping off the bus, the shopping center was just ahead.

    As I stepped off the bus, I saw the shopping center just ahead.

EFFECTIVE WRITING QUIZ 2 ANSWERS

1. It is necessary that you not be uninformed about this case.

    You must be informed about this case.

2. There is ample evidence which indicates that the attorneys for the defense did not provide inadequate counseling to their client.

    Ample evidence shows that the defense attorneys provided adequate counseling to their client.

3. Speaking and to listen well are important elements of communication.

    Speaking and listening well are important elements of communication. **OR**

    To speak and to listen well are important communication elements.

4. To win is the obvious goal, but playing fair is important too.

    Winning is the obvious goal, but playing fair is important too. **OR**

    To win is the obvious goal, but to play fair is important too.

5. They were charged with assault, robbery, and forging checks.

    They were charged with assault, robbery, and check forgery.

6. I remember his generosity and that he was considerate.

    I remember his generosity and consideration.

7. She worked quickly and in an efficient manner.

    She worked quickly and efficiently.

8. When working with power tools, eyes should be protected.

    When working with power tools, protect your eyes. **OR**
    Protect your eyes when you use power tools.

9. When changing a diaper, a baby should be on his or her back.

    When changing a diaper, lay a baby down on his or her back. **OR**
    Lay a baby down on his or her back when changing a diaper.

10. I have some letters the mail carrier delivered in my purse.

    The mail carrier delivered some letters that I have in my purse.

11. We have tuna casserole I made in the refrigerator.

    In the refrigerator, we have tuna casserole that I made.

12. Mollie came over while I was playing the piano with a piece of pound cake.

    While I was playing the piano, Mollie came over with a piece of pound cake.

13. While asleep, the flea bit the dog.

    The flea bit the sleeping dog.

14. I tried calling to tell you about that TV show five times.

    I called five times to tell you about that TV show.

15. Although very spicy, Dana managed to finish the enchilada.

    Dana managed to finish the enchilada although it was very spicy.

GRAMMAR MASTERY <u>TEST ANSWERS</u>

1. Some of the desserts **were** left by the end of the birthday party.

2. The papa bear thought that some of his porridge **was** missing.

3. Your brilliant excuses almost **make** up for your tardiness.

4. Neither Jackson nor Jenna **is** playing hooky. (CORRECT)

5. Neither Jackson nor I **am** playing hooky.

6. Either of us **is** capable of winning. (CORRECT)

7. All of the class **is** willing to take part in the prank. (CORRECT)

8. One third of the eligible population **tends** not to vote in national elections.

9. One third of the voters **tend** not to cast their ballots in national elections.

10. Here **are** the paper clips you requested.

11. She is one of those doctors who **make** house calls. (CORRECT)

12. Dr. Cresta is one of those professors who **do** whatever it takes to get **their** point across to **their** students.

13. She is the only professor who **does** what it takes to help her students learn joyfully. (CORRECT)

14. **She** and **he** are always fighting.

15. When Toni and **he** come over, we always have a great time.

16. It is **we** who must decide whether to tax ourselves or cut spending. (CORRECT)

17. Between you and **me**, this class is a joke.

18. **Who** do you think you are to give me advice about dating? (CORRECT)

19. **Who** makes up these English rules anyway? (CORRECT)

20. **Who** do you think should win?

21. **Whom** are you voting for?

22. **Whoever** has the keys gets to be in the driver's seat. (CORRECT)

23. We are willing to work with **whomever** you recommend.

24. The thoughts **that** Ted presented at the meeting were so worthwhile. (CORRECT)

25. The thoughts that Ted presented, **which** were about shifting national priorities, were well received.

26. When you do a job so **well**, you can expect a raise.

27. Bonnie was a **good** sport about losing the race. (CORRECT)

28. Harry smells **good**. What is the aftershave he is wearing? (CORRECT)

29. Lisa did so **well** on the test that she was allowed to accelerate to the next level. (CORRECT)

30. Our puppy is definitely **sweeter** than her brother.

31. With triplets, I have to be careful to divide everything equally **among** them or they will fight.

32. Karen should **have** known that her cheap umbrella would break in the storm.

33. Sometimes the **effects** of our generosity may seem minimal, but our good intentions do make a difference. (CORRECT)

34. Ben thought he had **laid** my jacket on that bench.

PUNCTUATION AND CAPITALIZATION <u>PRETEST ANSWERS</u>

1. Go **west** three blocks and turn right.
2. Yes, sir, I will do it immediately.
3. "How," I asked, "can you always be so forgetful?"
4. The woman who is standing there is his ex-wife.
5. Although we have a competent staff, bottlenecks do occur.
6. I did not receive the order; therefore, I will not pay my bill. (CORRECT)
7. We offer a variety of drinks, for instance, beer. (CORRECT. Comma after *instance* is optional.)
8. Is that book **yours**?
9. We have much to do; for example, the carpets need vacuuming.
10. Estimates for the work have been forwarded, and a breakdown of costs has been included. (CORRECT)
11. Because of his embezzling, the company went bankrupt.
12. A proposal that makes harassment of whales illegal has just passed. (CORRECT)
13. You may, of course, call us anytime you wish.
14. Paolo hurried to the depot to meet his aunt and two cousins.
15. Finish your job; it is imperative that you do.
16. Sofia and Aidan's house was recently painted. (CORRECT)
17. "Stop it!" I said. "Don't ever do that again."
18. I would, therefore, like to have an explanation for the missing cash.
19. "Would you like to accompany me?" he asked.
20. I have always had a mental block against **math**.
21. He is a strong, healthy man.
22. To apply for this job, you must have previous experience.
23. Marge, the woman with blonde hair, will be our speaker this evening.
24. He thought quickly and then answered the question in complete detail.
25. He asked if he could be excused.
26. It is hailing, not raining.
27. We will grant you immunity if you decide to cooperate with us.
28. You signed the contract; consequently, you must provide us with the raw materials.
29. I would like, however, to read the fine print first.
30. You are required to bring the following: **sleeping** bag, food, and a sewing kit.
31. The three **companies'** computers were stolen.
32. The **women's** department is upstairs and to your left.
33. It hurt **its** paw.
34. One of the **lawyers** left her briefcase.
35. "What does it take to become a licensed architect?" she asked.
36. I can't remember if her birthday falls on a Saturday, Sunday, or Monday next year.
37. I need to locate four states on the map: Arkansas, Ohio, Illinois, and Utah.
38. The clergyman who united the entire congregation was Unitarian.
39. The email read, "Hi, Camille. I haven't heard from you in two weeks."

40. The veterinarian said, "Unless **it's** bleeding and doesn't stop, don't worry about it."

41. To be able to let go of needing to discuss this with her mother anymore, Wendy decided, "This is her karma, not mine."

42. You must study hard to get good grades at a major university.

COMMAS QUIZ 1 ANSWERS

1. I took Angie, the one with the freckles, to the movie last night.

2. Jeremy and I have had our share of arguments.

3. You are, I am sure, telling the truth.

4. She left Albany, New York on January 18 of that year.
   (CORRECT. Comma after *New York* is optional.)

5. I need sugar, butter, and eggs from the grocery store.

6. Please, Sasha, come home as soon as you can.

7. Although you may be right, I cannot take your word for it.

8. We will grant you immunity if you decide to cooperate with us. (CORRECT)

9. I am typing a letter and she is talking on the phone.
   (CORRECT. Comma after *letter* is optional.)

10. She finished her work and then took a long lunch.

11. Mae said, "Why don't you come up and see me sometime?"

12. You said I could go, didn't you? (CORRECT)

13. To apply for this job, you must have a social security card.

14. He seems to be such a lonely, quiet man, doesn't he?

15. She wore a brightly colored dress. (CORRECT)

16. She has a good, healthy attitude about her work.

COMMAS QUIZ 2 ANSWERS

1. Girls who have red hair are very lucky.

2. He asked where his hat was. (CORRECT)

3. They are, one might say, true believers. (CORRECT)

4. Cheryl arrived in Denver, Colorado, hoping to find a good job.
   (Comma after *Colorado* is optional.)

5. On July 20, 1969, astronauts landed on the moon for the first time.

6. Life, liberty, and the pursuit of happiness are three guarantees granted to us by our forefathers.

7. I told you, Jesse, never to ask me that question again.

8. I may as well not speak if you refuse to even listen. (CORRECT)

9. I am already finished cooking, but he has not taken his shower yet.

10. I walked all the way to the bus stop and waited for a bus for over an hour. (CORRECT)

11. It is drizzling, not pouring.

12. What a delicious, appetizing meal! (CORRECT)

13. Dario drove to the airport to meet his wife and children. (CORRECT)

14. Yes, I can be ready in five minutes.

15. I will not stop you if you want to leave.

16. Rosie Hernandez, Ph.D., will be our guest speaker.

SEMICOLONS AND COLONS QUIZ 1 ANSWERS

1. You asked for forgiveness; he granted it to you.

2. We ask, therefore, that you keep this matter confidential.

3. The order was requested six weeks ago; therefore, I expected the shipment to arrive by now.

4. The American flag has three colors, namely, red, white, and blue.
   (CORRECT. Comma after *namely* is optional.)

5. Clothes are often made from synthetic material, for instance, rayon.

6. If you believe in magic, magical things will happen; but if you do not believe in magic, you will discover nothing to be magical.

7. The orchestra, excluding the violin section, was not up to par.

8. I have been to San Francisco, California; Reno, Nevada; and Seattle, Washington.

9. I need a few items at the store: clothespins, a bottle opener, and napkins.

10. I answered the phone, but no one seemed to be on the other end of the line.

11. I wanted a cup of coffee, not a glass of milk. (CORRECT)

12. You have won the following prizes, namely, a car, a trip to Hawaii, and a bathrobe.
    (Comma after *namely* is optional.)

13. If you can possibly arrange it, please visit us; but if you cannot, let us know.

14. I gave her a lot of money while we were married; hence, I do not wish to pay her a dime in alimony.

15. We have a variety of desserts, for instance, apple pie. (CORRECT. Comma after *instance* is optional.)

16. I needed only three cards to win, namely, the ten of hearts, the jack of diamonds, and the king of hearts. (Comma after *namely* is optional.)

17. I needed only three cards to win: the ten of hearts, the jack of diamonds, and the king of hearts.

18. I would, therefore, like to have an explanation for the missing cash.

19. Nature lovers will appreciate seeing whales, sea lions, and pelicans.

20. He has friends from Iowa and Nebraska, and Illinois is his home state.

21. We have set this restriction: do your homework before watching television.

SEMICOLONS AND COLONS QUIZ 2 ANSWERS

1. He has friends from Montana, Iowa, and Nebraska; and Illinois is his home state.
2. This is a difficult exercise but I am having fun. (CORRECT. Comma after *exercise* is optional.)
3. Although this is a difficult exercise, I am having fun.
4. This is a difficult exercise; I am having fun though.
5. The man who is wearing dark glasses is an FBI undercover agent. (CORRECT)
6. That FBI agent, who is wearing dark glasses, once protected the President.
7. Did you, John, eat my cake?
8. Did John eat my cake? (CORRECT)
9. Did his friend John eat my cake? (CORRECT)
10. Did John, his friend, eat the cake?
11. If everything goes according to plan, he will retire at 40; if real estate prices continue to drop, however, he may have to work until he is 65.
12. Golden retrievers, which are known to be gentle, are also loyal.
13. Dogs that are gentle are often good family pets. (CORRECT)
14. I would love to be rich and famous although fame has mixed blessings. (CORRECT)
15. I would love to be rich and famous, and famous is the first priority.
16. She chose the field of journalism because of Nellie Bly, the first woman reporter.
17. They built an adobe house but then they decided to move. (CORRECT. Comma after *house* is optional.)
18. They built an adobe house but then decided to move. (CORRECT)
19. They built an adobe house; however, they decided to move.
20. They built an adobe house because they decided never to move again. (CORRECT)
21. Since they moved to the desert, they decided to build an adobe house.
22. Mr. Liu held this belief: if he worked hard, he would be able to save enough money to travel to Madagascar and photograph rarely seen animals.

QUESTION MARKS, QUOTATION MARKS, AND PARENTHESES QUIZ 1 ANSWERS

1. He wanted to know when you will be here.
2. "Well," she said, "you certainly didn't waste any time."
3. "Is it almost over?" he asked.
4. "I've had it up to here!" she screamed.
5. The song asks, "Would you like to swing on a star?"
6. Carmen said, "She said, 'I'll never leave you.'"
7. She requested (actually she pleaded) that her name be withheld.
   (**OR** use commas instead of parentheses.)

8. This contract guarantees that we will 1.) deliver the merchandise, 2.) pay for all damaged goods, and 3.) make you the exclusive carrier of our products.
   (**OR** just use periods or parentheses after the numbers)

9. "May I have a rain check on that lunch?" I asked.

10. Do you believe the saying, "It is better to vote for what you want and not get it than to vote for what you don't want and get it"?

QUESTION MARKS, QUOTATION MARKS, AND PARENTHESES <u>QUIZ 2 ANSWERS</u>

1. "Correct me if I am wrong," she said.

2. "Correct me if I am wrong," she said, "but don't you usually drive a truck?"

3. Sandi asked, "Did Jeri say, 'I am pregnant'?"

4. I can have lunch with you tomorrow (Friday).

5. I hope you are feeling better. (I am sick today.)

6. Did he ask, "Where are my keys?"

7. Harry needs to know if he can count on you.

8. I smiled (actually I laughed) when I saw the expression on his face.
   (CORRECT **OR** you may use a pair of dashes or commas)

9. Nicole said with shock in her voice, "I can't believe what I just saw!"

APOSTROPHES <u>QUIZ 1 ANSWERS</u>

1. Her husband's wallet was full of curious, little items.

2. I went to my mother-in-law's house for dinner last night.

3. You may not enter Mr. Harris's office without his permission.

4. The girl's vitality and humor were infectious. (one girl)

5. The women's dresses are on the second floor.

6. It's a shame that had to happen.

7. It's hard to believe that winter is almost here.

8. Her mother and father's business went bankrupt.

9. It is his word against mine.

10. The actresses' costumes looked beautiful on them.

11. Sharon's arriving was unexpected.

12. The movie had its desired effect.

APOSTROPHES QUIZ 2 ANSWERS

1. His 6s and 8s looked alike.

2. Where would I find the men's room?

3. Both secretaries' vacations caused a delay in output.

4. New clients' accounts showed an 11 percent increase in sales. (*clients* is plural)

5. Most children's imaginations run wild when told that story.

6. Both sons-in-law's opinions were considered.

7. Several M.D.s agreed that one bacterial strain caused many of the symptoms.

8. These M.D.s' credentials are excellent.

9. Both brothers-in-law's jobs required physical labor.

10. Do you mind my looking at the earrings in this jewelry case?

11. Your right to privacy will not be abused.

12. Its beauty is unsurpassed.

HYPHENS QUIZ 1 ANSWERS

1. She jumped from a two-story building.

2. The show's cancellation was a real letdown. (CORRECT)

3. You must let down your guard.

4. You certainly have a go-get-it nature.

5. What a cute little bird she has! (CORRECT)

6. We offer around-the-clock coverage.

HYPHENS QUIZ 2 ANSWERS

1. Turn left after the big red door. (CORRECT)

2. This is a one-family dwelling.

3. Do you think he has above-average intelligence?

4. I would like that antique picture frame. (CORRECT)

5. She owns income-producing property.

6. That is a well-written letter.

HYPHENS WITH ly WORDS QUIZ 1 ANSWERS

1. This appears to be a firmly built house. (CORRECT)

2. A dimly lit restaurant can be rather romantic. (CORRECT)

3. A friendly little dog is all I need for company. (CORRECT)

4. The data was readily available. (CORRECT)

5. He is a happily married man. (CORRECT)

6. What kindly-looking eyes my grandfather had.

HYPHENS WITH ly WORDS QUIZ 2 ANSWERS

1. You are certainly a likely-looking prospect for the job.

2. A silly-acting child is a joy to behold.

3. A chilly, snowy morning would be a refreshing sight.

4. The lovely-sounding music came from that singer over there.

5. The friendly-acting dog growled whenever he had a bone nearby.

6. She appears to be happily married. (CORRECT)

HYPHENS WITH PREFIXES QUIZ 1 ANSWERS

1. antiaircraft

2. ultra-anxious

3. antidepressant

4. antifreeze

5. anti-impressionism

6. unpatriotic

7. nonprofessional

8. nonexistent

HYPHENS WITH PREFIXES QUIZ 2 ANSWERS

1. non-Jewish

2. preexisting

3. reestablish

4. self-satisfied

5. ex-Marine

6. anti-inflammatory

7. antiwar

8. unnatural

HYPHENS WITH re WORDS QUIZ 1 ANSWERS

1. When can we refurnish our home?

2. Our friendship was renewed.

3. I cannot recollect the story.

4. Please re-collect the papers, Mikaela.

5. That point should be reemphasized.

6. I enjoy re-covering chairs.

HYPHENS WITH re WORDS QUIZ 2 ANSWERS

1. The astronauts began the reentry phase.
2. Martin Luther began the Reformation.
3. I made a mistake and had to re-form the clay.
4. I must re-press the wrinkled suit.
5. I will re-lease the apartment after the current tenants leave. (lease again)
6. The couple was reunited after a long separation.

CAPITALIZATION QUIZ 1 ANSWERS

1. She said, "Bees are not the only insects that sting."
2. "You must understand," he pleaded, "that I need more time to pay you."
3. Mark Paxton, the vice president of the company, embezzled over one million dollars.
4. The President of the United States wields much power. (CORRECT)
5. I live in the northeastern part of the state where the climate is colder. (CORRECT)
6. The West, especially California, is famous for its cutting-edge technology. (CORRECT)
7. Have you read *All the King's Men*?
8. I enjoy summer more than any other season.
9. Employees of the company were laid off with little hope of returning to work.
10. My dear Mr. Simpson:
11. Sincerely yours,

CAPITALIZATION QUIZ 2 ANSWERS

1. I lived on Elm Street a few years ago.
2. The American River is extremely cold all year.
3. Do not swim in that river because of the swift current.
4. "You must realize," he explained, "that my circumstances are desperate." (CORRECT)
5. "Stop it!" she screamed. "Don't ever do that again."
6. She said, "We strive hard for a better world, but we don't lift a finger for perfection."
7. The West has a milder climate than the East.
8. You must take the following courses: history, geometry, and French.
9. The supervisor will decide whether state regulations prohibit our taking Monday as a holiday. (CORRECT)
10. My major requires that I take Calculus 1, history, and French.
11. The Federal Reserve Board will raise interest rates over many state agencies' objections.

PUNCTUATION AND CAPITALIZATION MASTERY TEST ANSWERS

1. I am asking if you would like to rollerblade together tomorrow.

2. Yes, Jean, you were right about that answer.

3. I read in a book, "If all else fails, succeed; if all else succeeds . . ."
   (CORRECT)

4. Wherever we go, people recognize us.

5. Whenever Cheryl is in town, she visits her sister.

6. Isabel enjoys the museum although she cannot afford the entrance fee.
   (CORRECT)

7. It may not be the correct part but I bet that it works.
   (CORRECT. Comma after *part* is optional.)

8. You are my friend; however, I cannot afford to lend you any more money.

9. Paul Simon sang, "I am a rock; I am an island."

10. At graduation, the principal said, "I believe that all of you are capable
    of greatness. . . . All of you have studied everything you need to succeed."
    (Two separate sentences with a missing sentence between them)

11. I asked Ella, "Did he ask for his ring back?"

12. John F. Kennedy, Jr., became a magazine publisher and a pilot before his tragic death.

13. Please contact me if you have any questions. (CORRECT)

14. The elections will be held on the first Tuesday of November 2008.
    (CORRECT)

15. The elections will be held on Tuesday, November 4, 2008, and the polls will be kept
    open until 8:00 p.m.

16. Carl worried about the hurricane but tried to stay calm and help his family. (CORRECT)

17. I favor green and yellow, and purple is her first choice.

18. I need to locate four states on the map, namely, Minnesota, Michigan, California,
    and Nevada. (Comma after *namely* is optional.)

19. This is the point that Einstein made: You cannot fix a problem with the problem.

20. Our philosophy teacher thinks that Einstein meant that we cannot stop war by waging war.
    (CORRECT)

21. A well-made argument was presented for negotiating a peaceful resolution. (CORRECT)

22. The argument for negotiating a peaceful resolution was well made.
    (CORRECT)

23. A liberally sprinkled dose of humor was very much appreciated.
    (CORRECT)

24. Our liberal-minded clergyman managed to unite the entire congregation.

25. Our clergyman, who united the entire congregation, was liberal minded.

26. Jan asked, "What did Joe mean when he said, 'I will see you later'?"
27. When I noticed that our dog cut **its** paw, I called the veterinarian right away.
28. Just to be sure, I called three more D.V.M.s' offices.
29. "You're right to be concerned," said one veterinarian. "I would like to take a look at your dog."
30. Even though it's 30 miles to the town where that D.V.M.'s office is, I wanted to take the drive.
31. The friendly-looking vet examined our dog's paw and suggested we have it bandaged.
32. We had pet insurance but still owed $40 in copayment fees.
    (CORRECT)
33. Our dog was a semi-invalid for a couple of days until she chewed off the bandage.
    (CORRECT)
34. I guess she did what any self-respecting dog would do by grooming herself.
35. The dog has fully recovered although I will never be the same.
36. I have learned that it's better to be proactive than to have regrets.
37. Wendy thought she knew everything about her mother but found out two years ago that her mother had been married before. (CORRECT)
38. When Wendy asked her mother about this marriage, Ilse (her mother) was hesitant to discuss any details. (CORRECT **OR** use commas instead of parentheses.)
39. "She will go to her grave with some secrets," thought Wendy.
40. "Do you understand her need for privacy?" Wendy asked her husband.